HENRY DAVID THOREAU

a reference guide
1835–1899

A
Reference
Guide
to
Literature

Joel Myerson,
Editor

HENRY DAVID THOREAU

a reference guide
1835–1899

RAYMOND R. BORST

G.K. HALL &CO.

70 LINCOLN STREET, BOSTON, MASS.

Library of Congress Cataloging-in-Publication Data

Borst, Raymond R.
  Henry David Thoreau : a reference guide, 1835–1899.

  (A Reference guide to literature)
  1. Thoreau, Henry David, 1817–1862—Bibliography.
I. Title. II. Series.
Z8873.B664 1987   [PS3053]   016.818′309   87-7420
ISBN 0-8161-8822-X

This publication is printed on permanent/durable acid-free paper
MANUFACTURED IN THE UNITED STATES OF AMERICA

Contents

The Author

Raymond R. Borst received his academic education at Hamilton College, the University of Rochester, the State University of New York, and Cambridge University of England.

Borst has blended a business career with his love for book collecting and writing. Over the years he has created a most complete private collection of Thoreau books and ephemera. His bibliographic research has taken him to the Bodleian Library at Oxford University; the British Library, London; the Bibliothèque Nationale, Paris; the Houghton Library at Harvard, and many other major collections.

His Henry David Thoreau: A Descriptive Bibliography, published by the University of Pittsburgh Press in 1982, is the standard reference work for collectors and booksellers. He is coauthor of The Parkman Dexter Howe Library: Henry David Thoreau and Ralph Waldo Emerson, published by the University of Florida in 1984. He is also author of many bibliographical articles on Thoreau and a contributor to several books on him.

He is presently a director of the Thoreau Society.

Preface

The plan of this bibliography generally follows that of the preceding ones of this series. It carries the writings about Henry David Thoreau from the first discovered notice of his name in public print through to the last day of the nineteenth century.

First, due credit must be acknowledged to those who have preceded me in this work. While little of this previous research has been annotated, it has given me a starting point on my four years of searching. John P. Anderson's listings in Henry Salt's 1896 revision of his Life of Henry David Thoreau has been most helpful, especially with the English articles. The most complete secondary bibliography is Francis H. Allen's A Bibliography of Henry David Thoreau, a standard reference since 1908. The Thoreau Society Bulletin, under the editorship of Walter Harding, has provided much of the source material. Great aid came from Kenneth Walter Cameron's volumes of reprints. All present and future Thoreau researchers owe him a deep debt of gratitude for his endeavors.

To record the notice Thoreau received from his contemporaries, I have listed all the references I could discover made to him in print during his lifetime. Subsequent to his death, only substantial statements about him are included. The arrangement of the bibliography is, first, chronological by year. Within each year, articles published each month, those in newspapers first, then those in journals, are followed by the books published during that year; the articles are listed chronologically, the books alphabetically by author. Reprints are noted at the end of the annotation. Where the reprint is dated prior to 1900, there is a cross-reference to the entry for it under the year of its publication. Where it is dated later than 1900, there is an author-date reference to the work containing it. Items I was unable to examine firsthand are indicated by an asterisk preceding the entry number; the source of the citation is given in the annotation. The abbreviations used for these sources and for the post-1900 reprints are as follows:

Allen   A Bibliography of Henry David Thoreau.
                                      Compiled Francis H. Allen. Boston and New
                                      York: Houghton, Mifflin, 1908.

ATQ	American Transcendental Quarterly (Hartford, Conn.). Edited by Kenneth Walter Cameron.
Cameron, 1958	Emerson, Thoreau and Concord in Early Newspapers. Edited by Kenneth Walter Cameron. Hartford, Conn.: Transcendental Books, 1958.
Cameron, 1973	Transcendental Log. Edited by Kenneth Walter Cameron. Hartford, Conn.: Transcendental Books, 1973.
Cameron, 1974	Response to Transcendental Concord. Edited by Kenneth Walter Cameron. Hartford, Conn.: Transcendental Books, 1974.
Cameron, 1976	Transcendental Apprenticeship: Notes on Young Henry Thoreau's Reading. Hartford, Conn.: Transcendental Books, 1976.
Cameron, 1977	Literary Comment in American Renaissance Newspapers. Edited by Kenneth Walter Cameron. Hartford, Conn.: Transcendental Books, 1977.
Cameron, 1980a	Transcendentalists in Transition. Edited by Kenneth Walter Cameron. Hartford, Conn.: Transcendental Books, 1980.
Cameron, 1980b	New England Writers and the Press. Edited by Kenneth Walter Cameron. Hartford, Conn.: Transcendental Books, 1980.
Cameron, 1981a	Table Talk. by Franklin Benjamin Sanborn. Edited by Kenneth Walter Cameron. Hartford, Conn.: Transcendental Books, 1981.
Cameron, 1981b	Further Response to Transcendental Concord. Edited by Kenneth Walter Cameron. Hartford, Conn.: Transcendental Books, 1981.
ESQ	Emerson Society Quarterly (Hartford, Conn.). Edited by Kenneth Walter Cameron.
Glick, 1969	The Recognition of Henry David Thoreau. Edited by Wendell Glick. Ann Arbor: University of Michigan Press, 1969.
Harding, 1954	Thoreau: A Century of Criticism. Edited by Walter Harding. Dallas: Southern Methodist University Press, 1954.

Harding and Bode, 1958   The Correspondence of Henry David Thoreau.
                          Edited by Walter Harding and Carl Bode. New
                          York: New York University Press, 1958.

Harding, 1971   Henry David Thoreau: A Profile. Edited by
                          Walter Harding. New York: Hill & Wang,
                          1971.

TSB   Thoreau Society Bulletin (Geneseo, N.Y.)
                          Edited by Walter Harding.

      Public and private collections form the basis for any bibliography.
The following have been most helpful in this work: the Cambridge
University Library, Cambridge, England; the British Library, London; the
British Library Newspaper Library, Colindale, England; the New York State
Interlibrary Loan System, which found many scarce items for me through
the efforts of Stephen Erskine, librarian of the Seymour Library,
Auburn, New York; and the staff at the Cayuga County Community College
Library. I am also deeply indebted to Marcia Moss and to the seat of
Thoreau knowledge, the Concord Free Public Library.

      Many scholars have contributed their time and talents to making this
book a better reference work. Walter Harding took me into his home for
several days at a time that I might research his tremendous Thoreau
library. He was always eager to share with me his seemingly endless
knowledge of Thoreau. Bradley P. Dean from time to time sent me
information on Thoreau's lectures that he had uncovered in his research.
I am deeply indebted to Joel Myerson, who encouraged me to undertake this
work four years ago. This book has benefited from his vast knowledge of
nineteenth-century New England literature. I thank Borgna Brunner, my
editor at G.K. Hall, and Hall's staff, for seeing this book through to
press.

      No bibliography is ever complete. The day it is published, it is
outdated. In 1885 R.R. Bowker prefaced the American Catalogue thus: "It
is the bibliographer who of all men has most occasion to realize the
imperfections of human endeavor. Completeness is an ignis fatuus that
eludes even the closest pursuit and the most painstaking endeavor."
Addenda and corrigenda are genuinely solicited.

Introduction

The years between 1835 and 1900 were turbulent for the literary reputation of Henry David Thoreau. Objectivity in viewing either Thoreau or his writings was rare until near the end of the century. Early in his lecturing as well as his writing career he was considered a copy of Emerson. The Salem Observer in reporting on a Thoreau lecture wrote that "in thought, style & delivery, the similarity was equally obvious." James Russell Lowell, in A Fable for Critics, derides him as only a shadow of Emerson. This opinion continued to be held by many critics for the balance of the nineteenth century.

Thoreau's manner of life early became an almost integral part of every evaluation of his work. Those who approved of his stern independence of spirit lauded him. Those who did not were on occasion often vituperous in their condemnations. It was impossible for some critics to separate the man from his writings.

The first strike at Thoreau's reputation came from his early mentor, in the words of the eulogy Emerson spoke at his funeral. While his talk was for the most part highly laudatory, he called Thoreau a stoic and felt that he could have been better than a captain of a huckleberry party. Emerson rewrote this and it was published in the Atlantic Monthly, where it increased the public's awareness that Emerson considered Thoreau cold and unreceptive to new ideas.

George Ripley, in the 13 June 1849 New-York Daily Tribune, called A Week on the Concord and Merrimack Rivers a "fresh, original, thoughtful work"; he liked his nature observations but was not delighted with the book's "Pantheistic egotism." The Spectator of London complained that the reader might expect a pleasant excursion, but it is filled with Thoreauian reveries. James Russell Lowell, in reviewing the book, gave it a good report and admired the prose but thought Thoreau "exaggerates the importance of his own thoughts." Many reviews followed in 1849 and 1850, some admiring, some concerned about his ultraheretical attitude, and some, as the Athenaeum of London, considering it "a curious mixture of dull and prolix dissertation." Godey's Magazine and Lady's Book for September 1849 praised it as clever and interesting but attributed it to John Greenleaf Whittier.

Introduction

In Walden; or Life in the Woods Thoreau's philosophy became more
integrated and better understood by the reviewers. Most approved the
book with quiet acceptance. Thoreau could now see his reputation
stretched as far as London to the east and California to the west,
where the Daily Alta California called it beautifully written with an
air of originality. Charles Frederick Briggs in Putnam's Monthly for
October 1854 questioned whether Thoreau actually liked life in the
woods, because he did not remain there. Much approval was given to
Thoreau's views on materialism. George Eliot, in a belated review in
Westminster Review for January 1856, stated that it contains a bit of
American life, not the "go-ahead species, but its opposite pole."

Many reports on Thoreau's lectures appeared in the newspapers of
the towns where he talked. The Waterbury American admired Walden but
felt that "as a popular lecturer [Thoreau] is evidently out of his
element." He gradually was considered a naturalist--one who saw the
beauties of nature and was able to write about those beauties. The
publication of his "Succession of Forest Trees" augmented this view.
He began to write to the Boston Society of Natural History on his
findings, and these findings were acknowledged in the Society's
Proceedings.

Thoreau's death on 6 May 1862 brought forth many printed eulogies,
poems, and reminiscences, most notable that of Emerson. In 1863
Excursions was published and received with mixed reviews. The Boston
Commonwealth hailed it as "the ripe fruit of serious thought," while
the New-York Times wrote that a nation of Thoreaus would return us to
Indian life. Others said that God did not design man to be a recluse.

The prose in The Maine Woods was found by some reviewers to be
dull but containing possibly helpful material for those who wish to
travel in Maine. The Continental Monthly stated: "Who among our
descriptive writers can surpass H.D. Thoreau?" Thomas Wentworth
Higginson in the Atlantic Monthly, admitting Thoreau's love of nature,
felt that his has "an occasional mistiness of expression."

The critics received Cape Cod cordially for the most part, but the
New-York Times saw little in Letters to Various Persons of interest to
anyone except those to whom the letters were written. The Boston
Commonwealth complained about the sparseness of personal letters but
agreed that the letters given are full of the spirit of the man. James
Russell Lowell in the North American Review of October 1865 made a
bitter attack on Thoreau's writings that, coming from this prominent
critic, did much to delay proper recognition of Thoreau's ability. He
claimed that Thoreau had limited and inadequate critical power from
want of continuity of mind. Again, however, he admitted that the prose
is of the best. Other reviewers rushed in to agree with Lowell. The
New-York Daily Tribune wrote that Lowell had a true perspective on
Thoreau with the illusionary veil of his supporters cast aside.

Introduction

Ellery Channing's <u>Thoreau: The Poet-Naturalist</u>, the first book-length biography, was published in 1873. Excerpts from the book had been printed in the <u>Boston Commonwealth</u> as early as December 1863. It is an unconventional biography, with anecdotes loosely linked together. The middle chapters do not have much relevance to the rest of the biography. Although it is written in a haphazard manner, it still has a wealth of interesting and valuable information.

Surprisingly, the next Thoreau biography was written by an Englishman, A.H. Japp, under the pseudonym of H.A. Page. It was published in America in 1877 from the advance proof sheets sent over from London, where it was published the following year. <u>Thoreau: His Life and Aims</u> "professes to be as Study only; an effort to gain a consistent view of the man's character rather than an exhaustive record of the facts of his life."

The third biography came from one who knew Thoreau well, Franklin Benjamin Sanborn, who lived at his house for a while and was well acquainted with all of his friends and neighbors. In 1882 he wrote <u>Henry D. Thoreau</u> for the American Men of Letters Series. In it he included many previously unpublished Thoreau letters, college themes, and other manuscripts, all grossly edited "to improve on Thoreau's style." The book, although a great source of information for Thoreau scholars, must be used with caution.

Thoreau's reputation had another hurdle to overcome, this time from England, in the form of an article by one of its most respected writers, Robert Louis Stevenson, in the <u>Cornhill Magazine</u> for June 1880. Lacking a complete understanding of Thoreau's philosophy, he condemned it as negativism. Many defenders of Thoreau took to the press to discount Stevenson's condemnation. William Sloane Kennedy in the <u>Penn Monthly</u> for October 1880 rebuked him for not considering Thoreau objectively. Perhaps Stevenson's harsh words contributed in their way to a restudy of Thoreau's writings in their own right.

In 1882 <u>Early Spring in Massachusetts</u> appeared, the first of the gleanings by season from Thoreau's unpublished journals, edited by H.G.O. Blake; three more were to come. Their reception was not spectacular. Thoreau disciples admired them, considering them excellent nature studies. Thoreau began to be compared to Gilbert White and Richard Jefferies for his close observation of nature. Henry Havelock Ellis, however, in his book <u>The New Spirit</u>, claimed that Thoreau was neither naturalist nor scientific observer, but merely a fairly intelligent schoolboy counting birds' eggs.

The best and most objective nineteenth century biography of Thoreau was written by Henry S. Salt, an English humanitarian and man of letters who became interested in Thoreau after Stevenson's attack. In 1890 his <u>The Life of Henry David Thoreau</u> was published after much research and correspondence with those in America with significant information. He revised the book and shortened it in 1896. He saw

Thoreau from across the ocean, away from any possible Concordian provincialism.

As the century wore on Thoreau became more and more prominently described in the many histories of American literature being written. He had been accepted at first as a minor, and finally as a major, American author. He took his place by Emerson and in some books ahead of him. No longer was he accused of aping Emerson's style. He had the distinctive Thoreau style, pure, and clear, and ageless. The appearance in 1892 of Familiar Letters of Henry David Thoreau, which included many family letters full of humor, gossip, and homely notes, overcame the rigidity of the 1865 letters and showed the reader a new dimension of Thoreau. At the conclusion of 1899, Thoreau was an established American institution.

Thoreau's Major Works
Published before 1900

1849 A Week on the Concord and Merrimack Rivers

1854 Walden: or, Life in the Woods

1863 Excursions

1864 The Maine Woods

1865 Cape Cod

1865 Letters to Various Persons

1866 A Yankee in Canada with the Anti-Slavery and Reform Papers

1881 Early Spring in Massachusetts

1884 Summer: From the Journal of Henry D. Thoreau

1888 Winter: From the Journal of Henry D. Thoreau

1892 Autumn: From the Journal of Henry D. Thoreau

1895 Poems of Nature

1899 Some Unpublished Letters of Henry D. and Sophia E. Thoreau

Writings about Henry David Thoreau, 1835–1899

1835

1 Harvard University, Cambridge. Order of Performances for
  Exhibition, Monday, July 13, 1835. Cambridge: Charles
  Folsom.
      Lists under no. 3: "A Greek Dialogue. 'Decius and Cato'
MANLIUS STIMSON CLARKE, Norton / DAVID HENRY THOREAU, Concord."

1836

1 A Catalogue of the Officers and Students of Harvard University of
  the Academic Year 1836-7. Cambridge, Mass.
      Lists Thoreau as a student.

1837

1 Order of Exercises for Commencement, XXX August, MDCCCXXXVII.
      Notes under "Exercises of Candidates for the Bachelor of Arts"
that "David Henry Thoreau" was one of three speakers at a conference on
"The Commercial Spirit of Modern Times, Considered in its Influence on
the Political, Moral, and Literary Character of a Nation."

1840

1 Concord Freeman, 14 February, p. [2].
      Prints a 10 January 1840 letter by Edward Jarvis of the
Kentucky Historical Society Library, Louisville, thanking the residents
of Concord who generously contributed books and pamphlets. Thoreau is
listed as sending ten pamphlets.

2 Advertisement. Concord Freeman, 20 March, p. [5].
      Advertises that the spring term of the Concord Academy would
commence on 23 March. John Thoreau, Jr., and "Henry D. Thoreau will
continue to assist in the Department of Languages."

1840

3 "Sympathy." Boston Morning Post, 4 July, p. 1.
     Reprints Thoreau poem from Dial.

4 Advertisement. Concord Republican, 20 November, p. [4].
     Advertisement for the fall term of the Concord Academy dated
18 September 1840 by John Thoreau, Jr., Receptor, stating that the fall
term of his school will commence on 28 September, Henry Thoreau
assisting in the Classical Department.The terms are: $4.00 for English
branches; with languages included $6.00. While pupils will be received
at any time, they must enroll for at least twelve weeks.

                              1842

1 Obituary. Concord Freeman, 14 January, p. [3].
     Reports the sudden death on 11 January 1842 of Thoreau's
brother, John, of lockjaw at the age of 27.

                              1843

1 "Concord Lyceum." Unidentified newspaper (6 January) clipping in
     the rear of Thoreau's notebook at the Morgan Library (M.A. 594).
     Announcement, 6 January, lists the lecturers for the 1843
season, including Thoreau. Reprinted in Cameron, 1958, p. 6.

2 "Concord Lyceum." Concord Freeman, 10 February, p. [3].
     An advertisement listing the Lyceum speakers noting that on 8
February Thoreau delivered a lecture on Sir Walter Raleigh and that
there will be a lecture every Wednesday evening at seven o'clock.

3 "Mr. Thoreau's Lecture." Concord Freeman, 10 February, p. [2].
     This lecture on Sir Walter Raleigh notes that he was a man of
many talents, including that of statesman, writer and soldier. He also
had many undesirable character traits, of which meanness and
selfishness were the most obvious. Comments that Thoreau presented the
story of Raleigh in a creditable manner. Reprinted in TSB, no. 75
(Spring 1961), p. 6.

4 Review of the April Dial. New-York Daily Tribune, 11 April, p.
     [1].
     The reviewer "rather like[s] these lines by Thoreau [followed
by his poem "Haze"] and also comments on Thoreau's translation from
Anacreon. Reprinted in 1843.5 and ATQ, no. 14 (Spring 1972), pp. 114–
16.

5 Review of the April Dial. New-York Weekly Tribune, 15 April, p.
     [1].
     Expanded version of 1843.4.

                              2

6 Review of the October <u>Dial</u>. <u>New-York Daily Tribune</u>, 19
   October, p. [1].
        Reads: "We have not room to speak of 'A Winter's Walk' by H.D.
Thoreau" (see 1843.4). Reprinted in part in <u>TSB</u>, no. 77 (Fall 1961),
p. 1.

7 ⸱ Excerpts from the October <u>Dial</u>. <u>New-York Daily Tribune</u>, 27
   October, p. [4].
        Prints two columns of excerpts from Thoreau's "A Winter's
Walk." Reprinted in part: 1843.8.

8 "Winter Scenery." <u>New-York Weekly Tribune</u>, 4 November, p. [1].
        Prints excerpts from Thoreau's "Winter's Walk." Partial
reprint from 1843.7.

                            1844

1 Review of the January 1844 <u>Dial</u>. <u>New-York Daily Tribune</u>, 25
   January, p. [1].
        Comments on Thoreau's "Extracts From a Lecture on Poetry, Read
Before the Concord Lyceum." Reprinted in 1844.2.

2 Review of the January 1844 <u>Dial</u>. <u>New-York Weekly Tribune</u>, 27
   January, p. [1].
        Reprint of 1844.1.

3 Advertisement. <u>Boston Courier</u>, 8 March, p. 2.
        Advertises Thoreau's "Reformers" lecture at Amory Hall.

4 Advertisement. <u>Boston Evening Mercantile Journal</u>, 8 March, p. 2.
        Same advertisement as 1844.8.

5 Advertisement. <u>Boston Post</u>, 8 March, p. 2.
        Same advertisement as 1844.8.

6 Advertisement. <u>Boston Courier</u>, 9 March, p. 2.
        Same advertisement as 1844.8.

7 Advertisement. <u>Boston Post</u>, 9 March, p. 2.
        Same advertisement as 1844.8.

8 Advertisement. <u>Lowell Journal</u>, 5 April.
        An advertisement by a classmate of Thoreau's, Charles W. Rice,
a commission merchant, giving him as a reference. Reprinted in <u>TSB</u>,
no. 142 (Winter 1977), p. 6.

9 Review of the April 1844 <u>Dial</u>. <u>New-York Daily Tribune</u>, 5 April,
   p. [1].

1844

"The Dial was filled with admirable papers by R.W.E., C. Lane, H.
D. Thoreau, and others. . . . The Dial has now closed its fourth
volume, and we have heard that it may not be continued. We hope
otherwise."

10 "Fire in the Woods." Concord Freeman, 3 May, p. [2].
      Relates the accidental burning of several acres of woodland
because of the carelessness of Thoreau and his companion. While
Thoreau is not mentioned in this article, it was an important event in
his life.

11 [ROGERS, NATHANIEL P.] "Notes from the Dial." Herald of
      Freedom,10 May, p. 46.
        Comments on Thoreau's "Herald of Freedom."

12 Comment on the closing of the Dial. New-York Daily Tribune, 18
      May, p. [1].
        Regrets that the publication of the Dial has been suspended
for the present and notes that it has been "sustained for three years
by the free-will contributions of R.W. Emerson, Margaret Fuller, W.E.
Channing, Theodore Parker, C. Lane, C.A. Dana, Henry D. Thoreau, E.
Peabody, and others of the deepest thinkers and most advanced minds of
our country." Reprinted: 1844.13.

13 Comment on the closing of the Dial. New-York Weekly Tribune, 25
      May, p. [2].
        Reprint of 1844.12.

1846

1 "Anniversary of West Indian Emancipation." Concord Freeman, 7
      August, p. [2].
        Reports that the antislavery women of Concord commemorated the
freeing of the West Indian slaves at their annual meeting held on the
doorstep of Thoreau's Walden Pond hut.

2 HAWTHORNE, NATHANIEL. Mosses from an Old Manse. 2 vols. New
      York: Wiley & Putnam, 1:19.
        Notes Thoreau's strange faculty for finding Indian artifacts.

1847

1 "American Literary Intelligence." Literary World 1:185.
        "Henry D. Thoreau, Esq. whose elaborate paper on Carlyle, now
published in Graham's Magazine, is attracting considerable attention,
has also completed a new work of which reports speak highly. It will
probably be soon given to the public."

4

2 CHANNING, WILLIAM ELLERY. Poems, Second Series. Boston: James
   Munroe & Co., pp. 157–58.
           Refers poetically to Thoreau.

                              1848

1 [GREELEY, HORACE.] "A Lesson for Young Poets." New-York Daily
   Tribune, 25 May, p. [2].
           Apologizes to Thoreau for publishing part of one of his
   letters without permission. The letter, written by Thoreau while
   living at Walden Pond, describes some of his life there. Greeley calls
   him a "thorough classical scholar, true poet." Reprinted in Harding,
   1965, pp. 213–14.

2 "The Backwoods of Maine." New-York Daily Tribune, 17 November,
   p. [1].
           Reprints extracts from Thoreau's "Ktaadn and the Maine Woods"
   published in the Union Magazine. Calls the sketches "quite superior to
   any description of wild-woods life that we have seen in several years."

3 "Salem Lyceum." Salem Observer, 25 November.
           Reviews Thoreau's lecture "Economy" and notes "we were
   reminded of Emerson continually. In thought, style & delivery, the
   similarity was equally obvious. There was the same keen philosophy.
   Even in tone of voice, Emerson was brought strikingly to the ear; and
   in personal appearance also, we fancied some little resemblance. The
   close likeness between the two would almost justify a charge of
   plagiarism, were it not that Mr Thoreau's lecture furnished ample proof
   of being a native product, by affording all the charm of an original."
   Reprinted in Cameron, 1973, p. 37.

4 Gloucester lecture. Gloucester (Mass.) Telegram, 23 December.
           Reviewer dislikes Thoreau's philosophy and his method of
   arriving at it, stating "his housekeeping was in rather a primitive
   style. Compared with this, Robinson Crusoe must have fared sumptuously
   every day. We know of no benefit likely to accrue to society from it."
   Reprinted in TSB, no. 125 (Fall 1973), pp. 6–7.

5 [LOWELL, JAMES RUSSELL.] A Fable for Critics. New York: G.P.
   Putnam, p. 32
           Lowell poetically derides Thoreau as only a shadow of Emerson
   by writing:

               "There comes ---, for instance; to see him's rare sport,
               Tread in Emerson's tracks with legs painfully short;
               How he jumps, how he strains, and gets red in the face,
               To keep step with the mystagogue's natural pace!"
   Reprinted in Glick, 1969, p. 3.

1849

1849

1 Names. February.
    Lists the members of the Town and Country Club, including
Thoreau. Reprinted in Cameron, 1973, p. 37.

2 Salem lecture. Salem Observer, 3 March.
    Reports that Thoreau's lecture on his life in the woods was
received with mixed opinions, some calling it "tomfoolery and nonsense"
while others "think they perceived, beneath the outward sense of his
remarks, something wise and valuable." The reviewer notes "in regard
to Mr. Thoreau, we are glad to hear that he is about issuing a book,
which will contain these lectures, and will enable us to judge better
their merits." Reprinted in Cameron, 1973, p. 37.

3 "The Lyceum." Portland (Me.) Eastern Argus Semi-Weekly,
    23 March.
    Reporting on Thoreau's lecture: "the subject was announced in
the papers as 'Home, or Domestic Economy' but the real topic was
'MYSELF-I.' The lecture was unique, original, comical, and high-
falutin. It kept the audience wide awake, and most pleasantly excited
for nearly two hours."

4 "Life in the Woods." New-York Daily Tribune, 2 April, p. [2].
    Reports on the lecture that "Mr. Thoreau is a young student,
who has imbibed (or rather refused to stifle) the idea that a man's
soul is better worth living for than his body." The reviewer also
feels that if more young men were to hear this lecture, "they would be
less strongly impelled either to come to New York or go to California."
Reprinted in Cameron, 1973, p. 37.

5 THOROUGH, TIMOTHY [pseud.]. "How to Live Mr. Thoreau's Example."
    New-York Daily Tribune, 7 April, p. [5].
    In a letter to the editor, a reader complains he is surprised
that the Tribune would endorse such a life as Thoreau was leading (see
1849.4). He thought that he might have missed the sense of the article
so he called in his wife to read it. She said that "the young man is
either a whimsy or else a good-for-nothing, selfish, crab-like sort of
chap, who tries to shirk the duties whose hearty and honest discharge
is the only thing that in her view entitles a man to be regarded as a
good example." Reprinted in Cameron, 1973, p. 42.

6 Editor's reply to "Timothy Thorough." New-York Daily Tribune, 7
    April, p. [5].
    Derides Mr. Thorough for taking the article on Thoreau to be
applied to all young men. The editor writes that "Mr. Thorough is
indeed in a fog--in fact, we suspect there is a mistake in his name,
and that he must have been changed at nurse for another boy whose true
name was Shallow. Nobody has proposed or suggested that it becomes

everybody to go off into the woods, each build himself a hut and live hermit-like, on vegetable products of his very moderate labor." Reprinted in Cameron, 1973, p. 42.

7 "Solitude Seeking." North American and Gazette (Philadelphia), 11 April, p. 2.
    This editor takes a contrary view to 1849.4, stating "the would-be hermit of Concord may or may not be a worldly-disappointed man: better for him that he were, than he should deliberately sit down in the woods, a Timon without cause, to reject and despise the common charities and duties, the pleasures and pains of life, among his fellow man." Reprinted in 1849.8 and in Cameron, 1973, p. 43.

8 "Solitude Seeking." Washington Daily National Intelligence, 19 April, p. 2.
    Facsimile printing of 1849.7.

9 Lecture. Worcester (Mass.) Palladium, 25 April.
    Reports on a Thoreau lecture, "Life in the Woods": "His lecture of 20 April 1849 was a history of his experience; and is said to have been witty, sarcastic, and amusing."

10 "Lake Philosophy." Worcester (Mass.) Palladium, 2 May.
    Reports on Thoreau's lecture at Brindley Hall continuing his account of his life at Walden Pond. Calls it "a mingled web of sage conclusions and puerility--wit and egotistical effusions--bright scintillations and narrow criticisms and low comparisons." He apparently strives to be eccentric. Thoreau reflects Emerson as the moon does the sun. Considers him one of "Nature's oddities."

11 Z. Review of Thoreau lecture. Worcester (Mass.) Daily Spy, 9 May.
    Tells Thoreau that he is "better as a woodman, or say, a woodpecker, than a cockney philosopher, or a city parrot mimicking the voices . . . of Emersons or Carlyles." States that the audience comes to be amused, not instructed in a better philosophy. Sarcastically asks him to give up lecturing for the good of all.

12 "Life in the Woods." New-York Daily Tribune, 13 June, p. [1].
    Comments briefly on Thoreau's life at Walden Pond. Reprinted in Youth's Companion, ed. Nathaniel Willis (Boston: Houghton, Mifflin, 1954), p. 903.

13 [RIPLEY, GEORGE.] "Mr. Thoreau's Book." New-York Daily Tribune, 13 June, p. [1].
    The reviewer praises A Week on the Concord and Merrimack Rivers "as fresh, original, thoughtful work . . . sadly rare in this age of omniferous publications. Its observations of Nature are as genial as Nature herself, and the tones of his harp have an Aeolian

1849

sweetness," but chides Thoreau's philosophy, "which is Pantheistic
egotism vaguely characterized as Transcendentalism, [and] does <u>not</u>
delight us." Reprinted in Harding, 1954, pp. 3–7.

14 Review of <u>A Week on the Concord and Merrimack Rivers</u>. <u>Holden's
    Dollar Magazine</u> 4 (July):448.
        Makes comparisons to Emerson's writings.

15 "Editor's Table." <u>Knickerbocker Magazine</u> 34 (August):177.
        "We propose, by-and-by, to follow Mr. HENRY D. THOREAU down
the Merrimack, even from Squam, Newfound Lake, Winnepisiogee, White
Mountains, SMITH'S-and-BAKER'S, Mad Rivers, Nashua, Souhegan,
Pitcataquoag, Suncook, Soncook, and Contoocook; but we haven't leisure
for the jaunt just now. Meantime, let us commend <u>A Week on the Concord
and Merrimack Rivers</u>, for which we are endebted to the publishers,
Messrs. JAMES MUNROE AND COMPANY to the attention of our readers."
Search of subsequent issues did not uncover a full review of this book.

16 "Thoreau's Travels." <u>Literary World</u> 5 (22 September):245–47.
        A review of <u>A Week on the Concord and Merrimack Rivers</u>.
Thoreau's attitude toward Christianity disturbs the reviewer but "apart
from the pertness and flippancy against which we would warn our
readers, Mr. Thoreau's is a readable and agreeable book." Facsimile
printing in <u>TSB</u>, no. 176 (Summer 1986), pp. 6–8.

17 "Mr. Herbert's Translation." <u>Boston Semi-Weekly Advertiser</u>, 29
    September, p. 1.
        Compares Herbert's translation of Prometheus's first soliloquy
with that of Thoreau and finds the former a "fair specimen of his work;
and [we] subjoin Mr. Thoreau's bold translation of the same passage
published some years since [<u>Dial</u>, January 1843]--as the nearest
approach we have at hand to that which it is not, a literally faithful
rendering of the original."

18 Review of <u>Aesthetic Papers</u>. <u>Literary World</u> 5 (29 September).
        Comments on "Resistance to Civil Goverment." "He appeals to
the New Testament, even; by which he means, of course, that part of
it which may coincide with his opinions. . . . This article is about
as fit in a volume of <u>Aesthetic Papers</u> as would be 'the voyage of
Gulliver.'" Reprinted in part in <u>TSB</u>, no. 168 (Summer 1984), p. 6.

19 "Editor's Book Table." <u>Godey's Magazine and Lady's Book</u> 39
    (September):223.
        Reviews <u>A Week on the Concord and Merrimack Rivers</u> and
mistakenly credits the authorship, writing that "those who have read
<u>Margaret Smith's Journal</u> will be at no loss in settling the authorship
of this clever and interesting work. Mr. Whittier touches all his
themes with the true poet's wand; all show forms of beauty and gleams
of light that, like the sunbeams on the far-off mountain, make the cold

and rugged landscape appear soft and charming." Reprinted in Glick, 1969, p. 223.

20 Review of A Week on the Concord and Merrimack. Spectator
    (London) 22 (13 October):975.
        Complains that the reader would expect "an agreeable series of excursioning incidents and descriptions of landscape in a half-reclaimed state," but "the bulk of the book consists of Mr. Thoreau's reveries that might have been written anywhere: they are rather flat and not of a kind of interest."

21 Review of A Week on the Concord and Merrimack Rivers. London
    Athenaeum, 27 October, p. 1086.
        Concludes that "the matter is for the part poor enough; but there are a few things in the volume, scattered here and there, which suggest that the writer is a man with a habit of original thinking, which with more careful culture may produce a richer harvest in some future season. The manner is that of the worst offshoots of Carlyle and Emerson."

22 FELTON, C[ORNELIUS] C[ONWAY]. Review of Henry William Herbert's
    translation of Prometheus of Aeschylus. North American Review 69
    (October):414.
        Compares this translation with that of his former pupil, Thoreau, whom he finds "a scholar of talent, but of such pertinacious oddity in literary matters, that his writings will never probably do him any justice."

23 Review of A Week on the Concord and Merrimack Rivers.
    Universalist Quarterly 6 (October):422-23.
        Comments on the good features of the book but adds that it is "interspersed with inexcusable crudities, with proofs of carelessness and lack of healthy moral discrimination, with contempt for the things commonly esteemed holy, with reflections which must shock every pious Christian."

24 Review of Lowell's article. Worcester (Mass.) Daily Spy, 6
    December.
        Does not have time to fully review the article but found it "a very amusing one, as might be expected from J. Russell Lowell, when reviewing Thoreau!"

25 [LOWELL, JAMES RUSSELL.] Review of A Week on the Concord and
    Merrimack Rivers. Massachusetts Quarterly Review 3 (December):
    40-51.
        Discusses Milton, Homer, Walton, and others in the early part of the review and then turns his attention to Thoreau. "The great charm of Mr. Thoreau's book seems to be, that its being a book at all is a happy fortuity. The door of the portfolio-cage has been left

1849

open, and the thoughts have flown out of themselves. The paper and types are only accidents. The page is confidential like a diary." While in general Lowell approves of the book he states "that Mr. Thoreau, like most solitary men, exaggerates the importance of his own thoughts," but he rates highly Thoreau's prose. Reprinted in TSB, no. 35 (April 1951), pp. 1–4.

26 Review of A Week on the Concord and Merrimack Rivers. Pictorial National Library [3]:60–61.
    Notes that "Henry D. Thoreau, a young philosopher . . . has published a volume of 413 pages. . . . The voyage was accomplished in a boat of home manufacture, equipt with oars, sails, etc., and loaded with provisions, cooking utensils, and a tent in which to encamp at night." Reprinted in TSB, no. 29 (October 1949), p. 4.

27 Review of A Week on the Concord and Merrimack Rivers. Unidentified newspaper clipping.
    Recommends the book as "worth while to read it, if only to see how rich the lives of some men may be." The reviewer objects to some of the religious philosophy, but says these pages can be skipped; aside from that, he writes, there is on every page "something so fresh and sparkling meets the eye." Reprinted in TSB, no. 130 (Winter 1975), p. 8.

28 Review of A Week on the Concord and Merrimack Rivers. Unidentified newspaper clipping in Sophia Thoreau's scrapbook.
    Predicts that the "numerous admirers of Carlyle and Emerson will read this book with a relish; for Mr. Thoreau writes in their vein, and to some extent in their dialect, and is a match for them in infelicitous conceits and amusing quaintness, yet he is not a servile imitator."

29 Review of A Week on the Concord and Merrimack Rivers. Unidentified newspaper clipping in Sophia Thoreau's scrapbook.
    Short uninformative review.

*30 R[OBINSON], E[LBRIDGE] G[ERRY]. Review of A Week on the Concord and Merrimack Rivers. Dedham (Mass.) Democrat.
    Reviewer recounts the happy days he has had fishing on the Concord River: "glad are we that the memory of 'The Shad' is perpetuated in so pleasant a book." He comments on nothing else about the book. Reprinted: 1877.13.

1850

1 "A Week on the Concord and Merrimack Rivers. By Henry D. Thoreau. London: imported by John Chapman, 142, Strand. 1849." Westminster Review (London) 52 (January):309–10.

1850

Reviewer commends the book in spite of "some rather long-winded disquisitions upon religion, literature, and other matters. . . . We shall be glad to meet our author again, as soon as his 'Day in the Woods,' which we see announced as nearly ready, shall have reached England." Notes that the English people are obligated to the "spirited" publisher who introduced the book to England. Reprinted in TSB, no. 59 (Spring 1957), p. 2.

2 COLLET, SOPHIA DOBSON. "Literature of American Individuality." People's Review (London), April, pp. 121–25.
    Reviews A Week on the Concord and Merrimack Rivers as an anti-Christian work stating that it "should be mentioned that our author's ideas on theology are ultra-heretical. The essay on Christianity is an expression of the freest pantheism. It is very original, sarcastic, pantheistic, and reverential. If anyone marvel how these qualities may be combined, let him read the essay." His digressions—which are essays on Eastern literature, Christianity, poetry, and friendship—are an added feature. Comments also on "Resistance to Civil Government," with long quotes from Aesthetic Papers.

3 "The Wreck of the Elizabeth." New-York Daily Tribune, 25 July, p. 4.
    Notes that Thoreau left Concord the day before for Fire Island to search for the effects of Margaret Fuller Ossoli.

4 "From the Wreck." New-York Daily Tribune, 26 July, p. 4.
    Reports Thoreau is still on Fire Island and Ellery Channing, brother-in-law of Margaret Fuller Ossoli, left Concord that morning to join him.

5 "Later from Fire Island." New-York Daily Tribune, 29 July, p. 4.
    A gentleman who had just left Fire Island advised the writer that Thoreau was still on the island searching for Madame Ossoli's manuscript on Italy "which is known to have reached the shore."

6 "Fire Island." New-York Daily Tribune, 30 July, p. 1.
    Notes that Thoreau returned from Fire Island on the Sunday before. He was not successful in his search for the manuscript or the body. He posted notices offering a reward for the recovery of either.

7 "Aesthetic Papers." Boston Courier, unidentified date.
    Remarks: "We must dismiss Mr. Thoreau, with an earnest prayer that he may become a better subject in time, or else take a trip to France, and preach his doctrine of 'Resistance to Civil Government' to the rest of the red republican." Reprinted in Cameron, 1973, p. 50.

11

1851

1 "Mr. Thoreau's Lecture." <u>Portland</u> (Me.) <u>Transcript</u>, 25 January
Reports on Thoreau's lecture on Cape Cod with: "He must be
heard to be enjoyed. In short, he is an original, who follows no
beaten path, but has struck out one for himself, full of winding bouts
and odd corners; perplexing labyrinths and commanding prospects, now
running over mountain summits, lost in the clouds, and anon descending
into the quiet vales of beauty, meandering into the deep recesses of
nature, and leading—nowhither!"

2 D[UYKINCK], E[VERT] A. "An Ascent of Mount Saddleback."
<u>Literary World</u> 9 (30 August):161–62.
Describes the Mount and relates Thoreau's comments in <u>A Week
on the Concord and Merrimack Rivers</u> with his own ascent.

3 <u>Proceedings of the Boston Society of Natural History</u> 3
(1848–51):383.
Mentions that on 18 December 1850 "Mr. Henry D. Thoreau of
Concord, Mass. was elected a Corresponding Member." Reprinted in <u>TSB</u>,
no. 73 (Fall 1960), p. 5.

1852

1 "New Publications." <u>New-York Daily Tribune</u>, 19 June, p. 6.
Lists the contents of the July <u>Sartain's Magazine</u> noting
Thoreau's "quaint essay on 'The Iron Horse' as being characteristic of
his musings."

2 "Authors in the August <u>Sartain's Magazine</u>." <u>New-York Daily
Tribune</u>, 22 July, p. 7.
Notes articles in this issue by "Thoreau . . . and others of
which any magazine will be proud."

3 FOSTER, DANIEL. <u>Liberator</u>, 27 August, p. 4.
In a letter to the editor [Garrison] on his visits with anti-
slavery advocates, Foster remarks on the beauty of Walden Pond and
states that the "hermit scholar who abode of yore in his humble cabin
by Walden Pond in Concord, would find rich materials in these pure and
placid inland seas for weeks of study, and a folio of reflections and
descriptions."

4 Announcement of forthcoming Thoreau lecture. Unidentified
newspaper.
States that Thoreau will lecture that evening at Cochituste
Hall on his life in the woods and believes "perhaps no man in the world
is better qualified from disposition and experience, to treat that

subject profitably. Conventionalisms have about as much influence over
him, as over a forest tree or the birds in its branches. And as with
his freshness of thought he unites a rare maturity of scholarship, he
can entertain anyone who is not muffled in more than ordinary
dullness." Reprinted in Cameron, 1973, p. 66.

5 Announcement of Thoreau lecture. Unidentified newspaper clipping
   pasted in Bronson Alcott's "Autobiographical Collections" for
   1852 (Houghton Library).
     "Mr. Thoreau will discourse this evening on Sylvan Life, at
the rooms in which Mr. Alcott had his recent conversations."

6 Listings. The Massachusetts Register . . . for the Year, 1852.
   Boston: Damrell & Moore, pp. 140, 145.
     Lists Henry Thoreau as a civil engineer on p. 140; his father
as a lead pencil manufacturer on p. 145.

1853

1 CURTIS, GEORGE WILLIAM. "Emerson's Club." Boston Commonwealth,
   19 May.
     Comments on the site of Emerson's home that it probably never
was the site of an Indian wigwam "nor has Henry Thoreau, a very
faithful friend of Mr Emerson's, and of the woods and waters of his
native Concord, ever found an Indian arrowhead upon the premises. . . .
If every quiet country town in New England had a son, who, with a lore
like Selborne's, and an eye like Buffon's, had watched and studied its
landscape and history, and then published the result, as Thoreau has
done, in a book as redolent of genuine and perceptive sympathy with
nature, as a clover-field of honey, New England would seem as poetic
and beautiful as Greece." Reprint: 1853.2.

2 [CURTIS, GEORGE WILLIAM.] "Ralph Waldo Emerson." In Homes of
   American Authors. New York: G.P. Putnam, pp. 233-54.
     Reprint of 1853.1.

1854

1 "Our Weekly Gossip." Athenaeum (London), 27 May, p. 655.
     Notes that Thoreau was a graduate of Harvard College and, "we
believe, was qualified for the ministry in the Cambridge Divinity
School. This vocation, however, he rejected for the more remunerative
occupation of a manufacturer of wooden pencils." He lived in the
neighborhood of Emerson, who "appears to have acted as 'guide, philosopher and friend' to a large number of nondescript geniuses with which
Massachusetts abounds. For some reason, which we hope he will explain
in his promised volume, Mr. Thoreau deserted his manufactory to inhabit

1854

a small hut by the wooded shores of Walden Pond, where he lived, as
near as was attainable, after the manner of the primitive race." The
result of his life at Walden was an almost "Calibanish familiarity with
nature." While there he wrote A Week on the Concord and Merrimack
Rivers, which the article considers "a curious mixture of dull and
prolix dissertation, with some of the most faithful and animated
descriptions of external nature which have ever appeared."
Reprinted in part in TSB, no. 168 (Summer 1984), p. 6.

   2 Prepublication notice of Walden. Boston Transcript, 21 July, p.
     1.

   3 [GREELEY, HORACE?] "A Massachusetts Hermit." New-York Daily
     Tribune, 29 July, p. 3.
        A digest of the forthcoming Walden prefaced by a two-sentence
introduction. Reprinted in TSB, no. 11 (April 1945), p. 3.

   4 [GREELEY, HORACE?] "A Higher-Law Speech." New-York Daily
     Tribune, 2 August, p. 3.
        In a preface to Thoreau's "Slavery in Massachusetts," the
editor questions whether Sumner, Seward, and Chase are genuine higher-
law champions but has no doubt that "Mr. Thoreau is the simon-pure
article." Reprinted in TSB, no. 11 (April 1945), p. 3.

   5 "New Publications." New-York Daily Tribune, 8 August, p. 1.
        Advertisement for Walden to be published the following day.
The same ad was run again on 9 August and in a smaller format on 10
August. Notes at the conclusion of the ad: "This striking and original
will be published in 1 vol. 16 mo. in cloth, at $1." Reprinted in TSB,
no. 11 (April 1945), p. 3.

   6 Review of Walden. Boston Daily Evening Traveller, 9 August, p.
     1.
        Comments that "it is a curious and amusing book, written in
the Emersonian style, but containing many shrewd and sensible
suggestions, with a fair share of nonsense." Reprinted in TSB, no. 160
(Summer 1982), p. 1.

   7 "Walden: ot [sic] Life in the Woods. By Henry D. Thoreau.
     Boston: Ticknor & Fields." Providence (R.I.) Journal, 11 August.
        Reviews the book in one paragraph ending with "as the
incidents were not remarkably stirring, he has filled up the pages with
his philosophy, which is shrewd and eccentric; and, altogether, the
book is worth reading, which is saying a good deal in these times."
Reprinted in TSB, no. 16 (July 1946), p. 3.

   8 "New Books / Walden; or Life in the Woods." Worcester (Mass.)
     Palladium, 16 August.
        Decides in this review of Walden that Thoreau can better

write about his life at Walden Pond than he can speak about it.
Considers Walden a prose poem that should be read and reread because
of the current tendency towards artificialities. Prints extracts from
the book.

9 Review of Walden. Portland (Me.) Transcript, 19 August, p. 151.
      Comments that the book is a revised and extended version of a
recent lecture, that it had the same "crooked genius." Agrees that it
has pleasant thoughts and some sound philosophy. "The book is the most
readable and original volume we have seen in a long time." Reprinted
in TSB, no. 160 (Summer 1982), pp. 1–2.

10 "Battle of the Ants." Portland (Me.) Transcript, 26 August, p.
      157.
      Prints an excerpt from Walden's "Brute Neighbors."

11 Excerpt from Walden. Portland (Me.) Transcript, 6 September, p.
      179.
      Reprints a passage from the chapter "Where I Lived and What I
Lived For."

12 "The Canadian Wood-Cutter." Albion (N.Y.) n.s. 13 (9
      September):424.
      Reprints an excerpt from the chapter "Visitors" of Walden.
Facsimile printing in TSB, no. 149 (Fall 1979), p. 1.

13 "New Books." Albion (N.Y.) n.s. 13 (9 September):429.
      A favorable review of Walden, calling it "one of those rare
books that stands apart from the herd of new publications under which
the press absolutely groans." Includes the complete passage of "The
Battle of the Ants." Facsimile printing in TSB, no. 149 (Fall 1979),
p. 2.

14 "The Lecture Season." New-York Daily Tribune, 20 September, p.
      [4].
      A list of thirty lecturers including Thoreau.

15 "New Book Notices." Daily Alta California 5 (23 September):264.
      A short review of Walden, commending it to its readers. Calls
it a strange story of the woodland life of a philosopher who lived a
Robinson Crusoe existence but "altogether besides being beautifully
written, it has an air of originality which is quite taking."
Reprinted in TSB, no. 131 (Spring 1975), p. 1.

16 [BAILEY, GAMALIEL?] Review of Walden. National Era 8 (28
      September):155.
      Calls the philosophy Emersonian and marked with genius and
intellect. "It contains many acute observations on the follies of
mankind, but enough of such follies to show that its author has his

1854

full share of the infirmities of human nature, without being conscious of it. . . . But, with all its extravagances, its sophisms, and its intellectual pride, the book is acute and suggestive, and contains passages of great beauty." Reprinted in Glick, 1969, p. 8.

17 Review of Walden. Graham's Magazine 45 (September):298–300.
        States that Thoreau is one of the transcendentalists "who lay great stress on the 'I,' and knows no limitation on the exercise of the rights of that important pronoun. . . . Occasionally he obtains a startling paradox, by the simple inversion of a stagnant truism. He likes to say that four and four makes nine, in order to assert his independence of the world's arithmetic." Notes that he has much of Emerson's quality of mind. In spite of the dogmatic approach of the book, however, the reader "will soon learn to pardon it for the real wealth of individual thinking by which it is accompanied." Reprinted in Glick, 1969, pp. 5–8.

18 Review of Walden. National Magazine 5 (September):284–85.
        The writer has just come across the proofsheets of Walden and is enchanted by them and cannot resist the temptation to copy them. This he does with quotations from the fourteenth and fifteenth paragraphs from the chapter "Where I Lived, and What I Lived For." Reprinted in TSB, no. 46 (Winter 1954), p. 2.

19 Review of Walden. Southern Literary Messenger 20 (September):
        575.
        Briefly notes that the book will please many readers with its "fresh rural scenes and descriptions of Mr. Thoreau, and his volume is a delightful companion for a loll under the rustling leaves of some old oak, far in the country. . . . We commend it to our readers." Reprinted in TSB, no. 46 (Winter 1954), p. 2.

20 Review of Walden. Watchman and Reflector, 5 October, p. 158.
        The weekly paper of the American Baptist Church comments that "beyond dispute [it] is one of the most original, eccentric and suggestive books which the season has brought out. The writer in relating his own experience, which he does with naivete, shows much power of reflection, and a philosophic knowledge of men and things." Reprinted in TSB, no. 160 (Summer 1982), p. 2.

21 STODDARD, ELIZABETH BARSTOW. "Walden; or Life in the Woods."
        Daily Alta California 5 (8 October):2.
        Review by a neophyte reporter who claims that Thoreau knew only a limited beauty. "The world of art is beyond his wisdom. Individualism is the altar at which he worships. . . . The book is full of talent, curious and interesting. I recommend it as a study to all fops, male and female." Reprinted in TSB, no. 131 (Spring 1975), p. 2.

22 "To the Editor of the Transcript." <u>Boston Evening Transcript</u>, 19
      October, p. 1.
        Reviews <u>Walden</u> and approves of Thoreau's disdain of
materialism. Feels "the influence which Mr. Thoreau exerts will not at
once spread over a large surface, but it will reach far out into the
tide of time, and it will make up in depth for what it wants in extent.
He appeals, with all the truly wise, to elements in our nature, which
lie far deeper than the sources of a noisy popularity." Reprinted in
<u>TSB</u>, no. 160 (Summer 1982), p. 2.

23 Review of <u>Walden</u>. <u>Boston Yankee Blade</u>, 28 October, p. 3.
        Reviewer is reminded of Emerson by Thoreau's philosophy, of
the Elizabethan authors by his quaintness and originality, and of
Gilbert White by his minuteness and "acuteness of observation. . . .
Almost every page abounds in brilliant and piquant things, which, in
spite of the intellectual pride of the author--the intense and
occasionally unpleasant egotism with which every line is steeped--lure
the reader on with bewitched attention from title-page to finis."
Reprinted in <u>TSB</u>, no. 160 (Summer 1982), p. 3.

24 BRIGGS, CHARLES FREDERICK. "A Yankee Diogenes." <u>Putnam's</u>
      <u>Monthly</u> 4 (October):443-48.
        Reviews <u>Walden</u> with a cynical eye, stating that Thoreau
probably tried his hermit life as an experiment and was happy when it
ended and he was able to return to his normal life in Concord, "for
although he paints his shanty-life in rose-colored tints, we do not
believe he liked it, else why not stick with it?" Concludes, however,
"There is much excellent good sense delivered in a very comprehensive
and by no means unpleasant style . . . there are but few readers who
will fail to find profit and refreshment in his pages."

25 PEABODY, A[NDREW] P[RESTON]. "A 'Critical Notice' of <u>Walden</u>."
      <u>North American Review</u> 79 (October):536.
        In a short paragraph Peabody commends the book and agrees that
Thoreau "says so many pithy and brilliant things" . . . and makes "so
many just comments on society . . . that his book is well worth
reading." Reprinted in <u>The Library of Literary Criticism of English</u>
<u>and American Authors</u>, 8 vols. (Bufalo, N.Y.: Moulton Publishing),
6:271.

26 Advertisement. <u>Providence Bulletin</u>, 5 December, p. 3, and
      <u>Providence Daily Journal</u>, 5 December, p. 3.
        "Independent Lectures / The Fourth Lecture of the Course will
be delivered in Railroad Hall, on WEDNESDAY EVENING, by Henry D.
Thoreau, (Author of Life in the Woods.) of Concord, Mass. Tickets for
the Course $1; Evening tickets 25 cents. For sale at the bookstores
and at Leland's Music Store, 165 Westminster Street. Doors open at 6
1/2. Lecture to commence at 7 1/2."

1854

27 Advertisement. <u>Providence Daily Journal</u>, 5 December, p. 3.
      Reprint 1854.26.

28 Advertisement. <u>Providence Daily Journal</u>, 6 December, p. 3.
      Reprint of 1854.26

29 "Independent Lectures." <u>Providence Daily Post</u>, 6 December, p. 2.
      Reminder of the Thoreau lecture that night, similar to 1854.26.

30 "Independent Lectures." <u>Providence Daily Tribune</u>, 6 December, p. 3.
      Reminder to the public that a lecture would be given that
evening by Thoreau, "a man of decided ability, who built his house in
the woods and lived five [<u>sic</u>] years on about thirty dollars a year,
during which time he stored his mind with a vast amount of useful
information, setting an example for poor young men who thirst for
learning, showing those who are determined to get a good education that
they can have it by pursuing the right course."

31 "Atheneum Lectures." <u>Nantucket Inquirer</u>, 13 December, p. 3.
      Lists the schedule of the coming lecturers with Thoreau for 28
December.

32 [CHILD, LYDIA MARIA?] Review of <u>A Week on the Concord and</u>
      <u>Merrimack Rivers</u> and <u>Walden</u>. <u>National Anti-Slavery Standard</u>, 16
      December, p. 3.
      Notes that these books are in striking contrast to the present
New England materialism, which the reviewer feels is greatly overrated.
Thoreau teaches that the main object of life is to <u>live</u>. While some
think that Thoreau's view of life is a selfish one, what he writes in
<u>Walden</u> under the heading of "Philanthropy" is the best defense against
this charge. To the frequent question: "What if everyone lived as
Thoreau did?" the answer is less wearisome gossip, more inspiring
conversations, less wearing out of body and soul to gain unneeded
material benefits. Thoreau feels that "the loftiest dreams of the
imagination are the solidest realities," while the affairs with which
men are busying themselves are "the merest froth and foam." Reprinted
in Glick, 1969, pp. 9–12.

33 Advertisement for Thoreau lecture. <u>New Bedford Daily Mercury</u>,
      26 December, p. 2.
      Notes that the lecture for that evening at the New Bedford
Lyceum will be given by Henry D. Thoreau, Esq., who is the author of
two books and several papers published in <u>Putman's Monthly</u>.

34 Advertisement for Thoreau lecture. <u>New Bedford Evening Standard</u>,
      26 December, p. 2.
      "THE LYCEUM--The lecture before the Lyceum this evening, will
be delivered by Henry D. Thoreau, a writer of considerable reputation."

1855

35 "The Lyceum." <u>New Bedford Evening Standard</u>, 27 December, p. 2.
    "We are compelled to omit from want of room, our notice of
the lyceum lecture last evening, by Mr. Thoreau of Concord. His
subject was "Getting a living." The lecture displayed much thought,
but was in some respects decidedly peculiar. We shall refer to it
again." [Search did not turn up a more complete review.]

36 Review of <u>Walden</u>. <u>Boston Atlas</u>, date unknown.
    "Strong thinkers, skillful anatomists of human impulse, would
be better occupied in seeking to assuage the troubles of the body
corporate, then in crossing to the other side and railing at it."

37 Review of <u>Walden</u>. Unidentified newspaper clippings in Sophia
    Thoreau's scrapbook.
    "The style is generally very pure and free from defects. We
should think <u>Walden</u> would become a favorite. . . . It contains
momentous truths and noble thoughts, forcibly and succinctly expressed,
and a searching analysis of the existing condition of society."
Compares Thoreau's writing with that of a Scotch writer, Hugh Miller.
"Whoever desires to either criticize or understand Mr. Thoreau, must
read and study his book carefully; and it will repay a studious
perusal."

38 BREMER, FREDRIKA. <u>The Homes of the New World: Impressions of
    America</u>. Translated by Mary Howlitt. New York: Harper, pp.
    166–67.
    Comments on the persons met in Concord during her American
visit. "F———[this is Thoreau. She must have misread her notes] went
out into the wild woods and built himself a hut and lived there———I do
not know on what. He also returned to common life, is employed in a
handcraft trade, and writes books which have in them something of the
freshness and life of the woods———but which are sold for money. Ah! I
wonder not at these attempts by unusual ways to escape from the torment
of common life. I have by myself made my attempts by these ways."
Facsimile printing of Thoreau excerpt, <u>TSB</u>, no. 54 (Winter 1956), p. [2].

1855

1 "Sketches of Atheneum Lectures." <u>Nantucket Inquirer</u>, 1 January
   p. 2.
   Extensive excerpts from the lecture "What Shall It Profit a
Man to Gain the Whole World and Lose His Own Soul?" Reprinted in <u>TSB</u>,
no. 166 (Winter 1984), pp. 1–3.

2 "The Connection Between Man's Employment and His Higher Life."
   <u>Worcester</u> (Mass.) <u>National Aegis</u>, 10 January, p. 2.
   Reports on a Thoreau lecture at Worcester on 4 January that
eventually was incorporated in his essay "Life Without Principle."

1855

3   "Suburban Letters." <u>Worcester</u> (Mass.) <u>Palladium,</u> 17 January.
        Notes that Thoreau in his recent Lyceum lecture "What Shall It
Profit," stated that he read but one newspaper and that took him a
whole week. Agrees with Thoreau's belief that newspapers contain a
large amount of trash. Considers it better for man to live in the
woods and learn from nature than to cut the trees and so make the
ground bare. Man should work for love of work, not for money.

4   ALGER, W[ILLIAM] R[OUNSEVILLE]. "The Transmigration of Souls."
    <u>North American Review</u> 80 (January):7.
        Reprints the passage on bullfrogs from <u>Walden</u>.

5   MORTON, EDWIN. "Thoreau and His Books." <u>Harvard Magazine</u> 1
    (January):87–99.
        Reviews both of Thoreau's books but gives more attention to <u>A</u>
<u>Week on the Concord and Merrimack Rivers</u> than to <u>Walden</u> and decides
that the latter is "less artistic than its predecessor, yet in other
respects superior, and in every way worthy the attention of all honest
readers."

6   RUSSELL, JOHN LEWIS. "Visit to a Locality of the Climbing Fern."
    <u>Magazine of Horticulture</u> 21 (March):126–34.
        Notes that the author was "introduced by Thoreau to the
aquatics which grew upon, and near, and <u>under</u> the stream."

7   "Town and Rural Humbugs." <u>Knickerbocker Magazine</u> 45 (March):
    235–41.
        Compares Thoreau' <u>Walden</u> with P.T. Barnum's <u>Autobiography</u>.
Reviewer is favorably impressed with <u>Walden</u> but calls Thoreau a rural
humbug and Barnum a town humbug.

8   "Battle of the Ants." <u>Boston Evening Transcript</u>, 9 August.
        Reprints the passage on ants from <u>Walden</u>.

9   "The Battle of the Ants." <u>Watchman and Reflector</u>, 9 August, p.
    125.
        Editor comments in publishing this selection from <u>Walden</u> that
it "has a moral to it worthy of attention."

10 PICTOR [pseud.]. "Massachusetts / Correspondence of the <u>Evening</u>
    <u>Post</u>." <u>New York Evening Post</u>, 13 August, p. 1.
        Comments on the reception of the Cape Cod natives to the
Thoreau articles on their region in <u>Putnam's Monthly</u>, many of whom took
offense at his description of them because they felt that "they are
quite as high in the scale of civilization as their neighbors are.
Their wild and solitary state is no hindrance to their advance in all
the graces and refinements of life."

11 "Lecture Season." New-York Daily Tribune, 19 October, p. 5.
    Announces the lecturers for the season, including Thoreau.

12 DUYCKINCK, EVERT A., and GEORGE L. DUYCKINCK. "Henry David
    Thoreau." In Cyclopedia of American Literature. Vol. 2. New
    York: Charles Scribner, pp. 653-56.
    Calls Thoreau "a humorist in the old English sense of the
world, a man of humors." Favorably reviews his two books and reprints
long extracts from them.

13 Proceedings of the Massachusetts Anti-Slavery Society at the
    Annual Meetings Held in 1854, 1855, & 1856.
    Reports in the statement for 1855: "In addition to the
speakers whose names have become more familiar to Anti-Slavery ears, we
had the pleasure, on the Fourth of July, to welcome HENRY D. THOREAU to
the public advocacy of our cause." Concerns Thoreau's lecture "Slavery
in Massachusetts," which he delivered at the Society meeting in
Framingham, Mass. Facsimile printing in TSB, no. 117 (Fall 1971), p. 7.

1856

1 ELIOT GEORGE [Marian Evans]. Westminster Review, American ed. 65
    (January):166-67; English:302-3.
    Belated review of Walden reading in part "we have a bit of
pure American life (not the 'go ahead species,' but its opposite pole'),
animated by that energetic, yet calm spirit of innovation, that
practical as well as theoretic independence of formulae, which is
peculiar to some of the finer American minds." Excerpts follow.
Reprinted in Glick, 1969, pp. 12-13.

2 ALGER, W[ILLIAM] R[OUNSEVILLE]. "The Literature of Friendship."
    North American Review 83 (July):104-32.
    Believes that the worthiest essay on friendship is contained
in the "Wednesday" chapter of Thoreau's A Week of the Concord and
Merrimack Rivers. It is "composition which everyone enamored of the
theme should peruse and ponder."

3 "A New England Town." Home Journal, 6 September, p. 1.
    Recognizes Thoreau as a naturalist but places his home in
Concord, New Hampshire. Reprinted in ATQ, no. 2 (2d Quarter 1969), p. 42.

4 "The Lecturing Season." New-York Daily Tribune, 10 November, p. 5.
    Announcing the lectures for the coming season, including one
by Thoreau.

5 "The Lecture Season." New-York Daily Tribune, 20 November, p.
    5.

1856

Announcing a list of possible lecturers for the coming season, including Thoreau.

6   GREELEY, HORACE. "The Bases of Character." In Rose of Sharon: A Religious Souvenir for MDCCCVII. Edited by Mrs. C.M. Sawyer. Boston: Abel, Tompkins, & Sanborn, Carter & Bazin.
    Extracts from a Greeley lecture, "Self Culture," in which while not naming Thoreau, he describes his Spartan life at Walden Pond. Uses his life there as a moral lesson for all. "Do not sell yourself even for learning. Plough, team, chop, or do anything to pay your way, and be twice as long acquiring it, rather than borrow it." Be an individual in all ways. TSB, no. 116 (Summer 1971), pp. 5–7.

7   LOWELL, Mrs. ANNA C. Seed-Grain for Thought and Discussion. 2 vols. Boston: Ticknor & Fields, 1:360 pp.; 2:307 pp.
    Contains many passages from Thoreau's writings.

8   Proceedings of the Boston Society of Natural History 5 (1854–56):86.
    Notes that Thoreau presented the Society with copies of his two books some time near the close of 1854.

1857

1   "Henry D. Thoreau`s Lecture." Worcester (Mass.) Daily Spy, 11 February, p. 2.
    Reports on Thoreau's lecture on "The Wild" at Fitchburg the week before and notes that it will be repeated the next Friday evening at Brinley Hall. The lecture is "the deep, rich outpouring of the author's life and genius, and not something got up for the occasion. . . . His words will surely be remembered when most of our literature is forgotten." Reprinted in Concord Saunterer, no. 2 (August 1984), p. 45.

2   "Henry D. Thoreau's Lecture." Fitchburg (Mass.) Sentinel, 13 February.
    Reports favorably on Thoreau's lecture on walking.

3   Review of Sylvester Judd's Margaret. North American Review 84 (April):554–55.
    In this novel Emerson says: "He found a consistent interpreter in his young disciple, Thoreau, the hermit of Walden Pond who gave up the world for nature and himself," and then notes the cost of the house and annual cost of living.

4   Thoreau's visit to New Bedford. New Bedford Mercury, ? April.
    Newspaper clipping in Bronson Alcott's journal.

1858

Notes Thoreau's visit to Ricketson of New Bedford in the social column and describes him as "well-known on reforms and literature."

5 "The Lecture Season." New-York Daily Tribune, 18 September, p. 5.
    A list of fifty-six names of persons "who lectured with acceptance last winter and are ready to do so this season," including Thoreau.

6 "An American Diogenes." Chamber's Journal 8 (21 November):330-32.
    Reviews Walden with a view not of the ancient cynicism of Diogenes but rather with the modern interpretation of the word. Notes that Thoreau tried teaching school without success; tried business but found that "it curses everything it handles"; tried "doing good" but found that it did not agree with his constitution so he borrowed an axe, built a hut and squatted another's land. "The natural sights and sounds of the woods, as described by Mr. Thoreau, form much pleasanter reading than his vague and scarcely comprehensible social theories." Finally, the reviewer is reminded of Barnum. Neither cares for hard work; "but while one prefers diminishing his wants, the other, increasing them, invents extraordinary schemes for their gratification" (see 1855.7). Reprinted in Harding, 1954, pp. 12-21.

7 MELVILLE, HERMAN. The Confidence Man: His Masquerade. New York: Dix, Edwards, pp. 394.
    The character, Egbert S. Oliver, of this novel is believed to be a caricature of Thoreau. Sections of Thoreau's writings are satirized.

1858

1 Report by Boston Correspondent. New-York Daily Tribune, 21 May, p. 5.
    Reports that the June Atlantic Monthly will contain an unsigned article entitled "Chesuncook" that is obviously the work of Thoreau.

2 "A White Mountain Excursion." New-York Daily Tribune, 17 July, p. 6.
    Reports on Thoreau's excursion to the White Mountains with George F. Hoar.

3 "The Lecture Season." New-York Daily Tribune, 12 October, p. 5.
    Lists over one hundred names of those desiring to give lectures, including Thoreau. Reprinted in Cameron, 1973, p. 128.

23

1858

4 CHANNING, WILLIAM ELLERY. Near Home: A Poem. Boston: James
   Munroe & Co., pp. 3–6, 30–31.
      The book is dedicated to Thoreau and has poetic references to
him.

5 RICKETSON, DANIEL. The History of New Bedford. New Bedford:
   Published by the author, pp. 126–29.
      Describes Thoreau's trip of 27 June with Ricketson to Naushon,
one of the Elizabeth Islands off the coast of New Bedford. While
Thoreau is identified only as a "congenial friend," Thoreau's journal
for that day also describes the island visit. He notes the various
kinds of vegetation on the island.

1859

1 "Reading." Massachusetts Teacher 12 (January):20–24.
      Reprints this chapter from Walden.

2 Harvard College / Committees of Examination. Form letter dated
   28 March.
      Notifies Thoreau that he has been appointed a member of the
"Committee for Examination in Natural History."

3 Second course of the projected lecture season at Frazier's Hall,
   Lynn, Massachusetts. Lynn (Mass.) Weekly Reporter, 9 April, p.
   2.
      Lists Thoreau to speak on "Autumnal Tints" on 3 May. (Starr
King asked to have his lecture date changed; as a result Thoreau
lectured on 26 April in place of his scheduled date.)   Reprinted in
ATQ, no. 24, pt. 4 (Spring 1972), pp. 158–59.

4 "Frazier Hall Lectures." Lynn (Mass.) Weekly Reporter, 30 April,
   p. 2.
      Reports on Thoreau's Lynn lecture; "Autumnal Tints": "It is
utterly useless for us to attempt to give anything like a sketch of the
lecture. We fear that it would be dryer than the dry leaves talked or
(rather read) about, and in which he saw so much poetry and beauty."
In closing, Thoreau suggested that the listeners train their eyes to
appreciate the beauties of nature that generally go unnoticed. For the
most part, the lecture was enjoyed. Reprinted in ATQ, no. 14, pt. 4
(Spring 1972), pp. 161–63.

5 "Lyceum Lecturers." New-York Daily Tribune, 9 September, p. 3.
      Thoreau is included in a list of 194 persons who are ready for
lecture engagements. Reprinted in Cameron, 1973, p. 133.

6 Unidentified clipping in Bronson Alcott's journal following his
   2 October entry.

"Henry D. Thoreau, of Concord, will speak to the Twenty-Eighth Congregational Society, tomorrow forenoon, at Music Hall, 'Misspent Lives.'"

7 Advertisement. Boston Evening Transcript, 8 October, p. 2.
"Rev. Theodore Parker's congregation will be addressed tomorrow forenoon, at Music Hall, by Henry D. Thoreau, on 'Misspent Lives.'"

8 Lecture announcement. Boston Daily Traveller, 8 October, p. 2.
"HENRY D. THOREAU, of Concord, will speak to the Twenty-Eighth Congregational Society tomorrow forenoon, at the Music Hall. 'Misspent Lives.'"

9 "A Hermit in the Pulpit / An Address on Misspent Lives." Boston Atlas and Daily Bee, 10 October, p. 2.
Reports on Thoreau's Music Hall lecture of 9 October entitled "The Way in Which We Spend Our Lives," which was listened "to the close with interest. . . . We have merely made a note or two of the lecture, which was singular, but in some respects, an able production."

10 "Personal." New-York Daily Tribune, 12 October, p. 6.
Reviews Thoreau's lecture, "Misspent Lives," given at the Music Hall in Boston on 9 October, calling it "original, racy and erratic."

11 "Boston and Vicinity." Unidentified newspaper clipping [October?] cut out by Daniel Ricketson and pasted in his copy of Walden.
Reporter calls Thoreau "a model cynic of modern times," writes of his delivery that "he has a fine voice, and a prompt, effective style of oratory that fixes the attention of the hearer." This is followed by his interpretation of some of Thoreau's remarks. Reprinted in TSB, no. 105 (Fall 1968), p. 7.

12 "Henry D. Thoreau at Music Hall." Banner of Light, ? October. Undated newspaper clipping in vol. 8 of Alcott's "Autobiographical Collections."
Reports in detail on the lecture and concludes that "the lecture, notwithstanding its very peculiar views, elicited much interest from the epigrammatic style in which it was clothed." Reprinted in TSB, no. 170 (Winter 1985), pp. 4–5.

13 "Fraternity Lectures." Boston Journal, 1 November.
Reports that Thoreau gave the fifth lecture at the Tremont Temple because the scheduled speaker, Frederick Douglass, could not be there. He gave his talk on John Brown. Reprinted in Cameron, 1973, p. 134.

1859

14   "Fraternity Lectures." Boston Atlas and Daily Bee, 2 November.
       Reviews Thoreau's lecture on John Brown and notes that it
"presents the views of a fanatic in relation to John Brown's Virginia
war, and, as well might be expected they are extreme enough." The
lecture is reprinted in 1860.16.

15   "Fifth Fraternity Lecture." Liberator, 4 November, p. 174.
       When the scheduled speaker, Frederick Douglass, did not show
to give his lecture on "Self-Made Man" because of threats on his life,
Thoreau volunteered his services and spoke on "John Brown of
Ossawattomie." "This exciting theme seemed to have awakened 'the
hermit of Concord' from his usual state of philosophical indifference,
and he spoke with enthusiasm for an hour and a half." Thoreau censured
the press including the Liberator, for not being active enough in
behalf of John Brown's cause. The reporter took exception to this,
stating that the Liberator's editor, Garrison, had "bestowed hearty
praise upon the enterprise at Harper's Ferry."

16   "Fraternity Lectures." New York Herald, 5 November, p. 2.
       Reprint of 1859.14. Reprinted in Cameron, 1981, pt. 2, pp.
32-33.

17   "From Boston." New-York Daily Tribune, 9 November, p. 3.
       Reports on Thoreau's lecture on John Brown given at the
Tremont Temple the Tuesday before. "There were some just and striking
remarks in it, and many foolish and ill-natured ones. Sneers at the
Republicans were quite frequent."

18   "Meeting to Aid John Brown's Family." Unidentified newspaper
       clipping in Bronson Alcott's journal (19 November).
       "Selections from Brown's writings, and others, were offered by
R.W. Emerson, H.D. Thoreau, I. [sic] S. Keyes, Charles Bowers, and A.B.
Alcott."

19   "Brown in the Boston Churches." New York Evening Express, 6
       December.
       "The services were commenced with the singing by the congrega-
tion of the following hymn, from the pen of a young gentleman from
Concord, supposed to be Mr. Thoreau."

20   Proceedings of the Boston Society of Natural History 6 (1856-
       59):430, 431.
       Reports that on 15 December 1858 the "Specimens of Pomotis and
Esox, of the amphibians, were presented by Mr. H.D. Thoreau, from
Concord, Mass. Mr. Putnam was of the opinion that one of the Pomotis
would prove a new species." And "Donations to Museum. . . . December
15. Specimens of young Pomotis, Esox, and frogs, from Concord, Mass.,
by H.D. Thoreau."

1860

1 "Walden Woods." Dial (Cincinnati) 1 (February):101.
   Verse.

2 "Walden Water." Dial (Cincinnati) 1 (February):102.
   Verse.

3 "Mr. Sanborn's Case." Boston Journal, 4 April.
   Reports on a meeting to celebrate the rescue of Frank Sanborn from the federal authorities who sought him because of his anti-
slavery activities. Several townspeople spoke, including Thoreau, who
advocated resistance to unjust laws. Reprinted in TSB, no. 72 (Summer
1961), p. 4.

4 "New Publications." New-York Daily Tribune, 9 May, p. 1.
   An advertisement notes the publication of Redpath's Echoes of
Harper's Ferry, with mention of Thoreau's speeches contained in it.

5 REDPATH, JAMES. "The American Insurrection." Liberator, 29
   June, p. 2.
   Notice of the meeting at North Elba, N.Y., on 4 July
1860 to celebrate John Brown and his principles with a list of the
invited guests, which included Thoreau.

6 "Literature and Agriculture." Cincinnati Daily Gazette, 7 July.
   Notes that a person like Thoreau, "a philosophical vagabond,"
is more valuable to the world than a hundred farmers for "any plodder
can raise beans, but it is only one in a million who can write a
readable volume."

7 Report on the John Brown Memorial Celebration. Liberator, 27
   July, p. 118.
   Reports on the proceedings at North Elba on 4 July. Thoreau
was not present. His speech was read by the secretary of the meeting,
R.J. Hinton.

8 Announcement of Thoreau lecture. Lowell (Mass.) Weekly Journal,
   7 September, p. 2.
   Notes that Thoreau will speak the next Sunday at Welles Hall;
that he is the author of several books and a contributor to the
Atlantic Monthly; and that he lived "one year solitary and alone, on
the shore of Walden Pond." The lecture to be before the Spiritualist
Congregation. "We do not known [sic], however, that Thoreau is a
Spiritualist; rather think that he is not."

9 Advertisement. Lowell (Mass.) Daily Citizen, 8 September, p. 2.
   "Mr. Henry D. Thoreau, the naturalist, will lecture at Welles
Hall tomorrow forenoon and afternoon."

1860

10 Advertisement. <u>Lowell</u> (Mass.) <u>Daily Journal and Courier</u>, 8
September, p. 2.
"Henry D. Thoreau, a gentleman of marked ability and great
originality, will speak at Welles Hall tomorrow forenoon and
afternoon."

11 "Lyceum Lectures." <u>New-York Daily Tribune</u>, 27 October, p. 5.
List seventy lecturers including Thoreau.

12 "Works of James Redpath." <u>New-York Daily Tribune</u>, 9 November, p.
1.
A short review of Redpath's <u>Echoes of Harper's Ferry</u>,
concluding with: "The services at Concord composed by Emerson, Thoreau,
Alcott and Sanborn, etc. unsurpassed in beauty even by the Book of
Common Prayer."

13 "Institute Lecture." <u>Waterbury</u> (Conn.) <u>American</u>, 14 December.
Reports on Thoreau's lecture on "Autumnal Tints" at the
Waterbury Young Men's Institute. Notes that he is the author of two or
three books and one, "Life in the Woods has passed though several
editions and has a high reputation"; however, "as a popular lecturer he
is evidently out of his element, in fact as Artemus Ward would say,
lecturing is not his 'forte.'"

14 HAWTHORNE, NATHANIEL. <u>The Marble Fawn</u>. 2 vols. Boston:
Ticknor & Fields, 1:283 pp.; 2:284 pp.
The character of Donatello in this novel is thought by some to
be modeled after Thoreau.

15 REDPATH, JAMES. "Dedication." In <u>The Public Life of John Brown</u>.
Boston: Thayer & Eldridge, p. 191.
Dedicated to "Wendell Phillips, Ralph Waldo Emerson and Henry
D. Thoreau, Defenders of the Faithful, Who when the Mob Shouted
'Madman!' Said 'Saint!'" States that Thoreau called Brown a "true
Transcendentalist."

16 REDPATH, JAMES. "Lecture by Henry D. Thoreau." In <u>Echoes of
Harper's Ferry</u>. Boston: Thayer & Eldridge, pp. 17–42.
Prints Thoreau's lecture given at Concord, Sunday evening, 30
October 1859 and reviews in 1859.14.

17 <u>Transactions of the Middlesex Agricultural Society for the Year
1860</u>. Concord: Benjamin Tolman, pp. 8–20.
Prints the "Succession of Forest Trees" address given by
Thoreau before the Society on 20 September with the comment "the
President, . . . after a few remarks, introduced to the audience Mr.
Henry David Thoreau, who delivered a fine address. At the close of the
brief address of Mr. Thoreau, Gov. Boutwell, President of the Society,

congratulated the audience that they had heard an address so plain and practical, and at the same time showing such close observation, and careful study of natural phenomenon." Reprinted in Eighth Annual Report of the Secretary of the Massachusetts Board of Agriculture, pp. 11-23. Some humorous passages are omitted in this reprinting.

1861

1 F., R.J. "Society Report--Succession of Forest Trees." New England Farmer 13 (February):89-90.
    A digest of Thoreau's speech before the Middlesex Society (see 1860.16). Reprinted in TSB, no. 143 (Spring 1978), p. 6.

2 "Middlesex Agricultural Society." New England Farmer 13 (February):91.
    Reviews 1860.16 and notes that Thoreau's speech is given in full.

3 "A Week on the Frontier." Minneapolis State Atlas, 3 July.
    Reports on the group who visited the Sioux Indians in Minnesota. Among the "very choice and select company" was "Henry D. Thoreau, Esq., the celebrated abolitionist." Reprinted in TSB, no. 56 (Fall 1956), pp. 2-4.

4 ARGOS [pseud.]. "From Concord." New-York Daily Tribune, 30 July, p. 6.
    After describing the Concord battlefield the reporter remarks: "I am sorry to say that the excellent naturalist and poet, Henry D. Thoreau, is in poor health."

5 [HIGGINSON, THOMAS WENTWORTH.] "My Outdoor Study." Atlantic Monthly 8 (September):302-9.
    Discusses the beauties of nature and those who wrote best about her. Eliminates Emerson and Ruskin. Picks "an odd triad . . . Wordsworth, Bettine Brentino, and Thoreau." States that Thoreau "shows us that absolutely nothing in Nature has ever yet been described,--not a bird nor a berry of the woods, nor a drop of water, nor a spinula of ice, nor summer, nor winter, nor sun, nor star."

6 Proceedings of the Boston Society of Natural History 7 (1859-61):355, 430.
    Reports that "A letter was read from Mr. H.D. Thoreau, of Concord, Mass., in reference to a Canada lynx (Lynx Canadensis), killed in Carlisle, Mass. Sept. 9, 1860." The letter was read on 17 October 1860. Also notes "Books received during the quarter ending December 31, 1860. . . . Transactions of the Middlesex Agricultural Society for 1860. 8vo. Concord, 1860. From H. D. Thoreau." Reprinted in TSB,

1861

no. 73 (Fall 1960), p. 5. The letter referred to is reprinted in TSB,
no. 15 (April 1946), pp. 1-2.

1862

1 [LOWELL, JAMES RUSSELL.] "Mason and Sidell: A Yankee Idyll."
   Atlantic Monthly 9 (February):259.
        Poetically refers to the village of Concord:
        "But nowadays the Bridge ain't what they show,
        So much ez Em'son, Hawthorne, an' Thoreau."

2 [ALCOTT, AMOS BRONSON.] "The Forester." Atlantic Monthly 9
   (April):443-45.
        Alcott portrays Thoreau as "a son of Nature" who is also a
"peripatetic philosopher" who is "perhaps a little overconfident
sometimes, and stiffly individual, dropping society clean out of his
theories." Reprinted in facsimile in TSB, no. 78 (Winter 1962), pp. 2-
3.

3 E[MERSON, RALPH WALDO]. "Obituary." Boston Daily Advertiser, 8
   May, p. 109.
        Obituary for Thoreau. Reprinted as "Henry D. Thoreau.
Emerson's Obituary" (Lakeland, Mich.: Edwin B. Hill, 1904), 10 pp.

4 [CHANNING, WILIAM ELLERY.] "Stanzas: Written to be sung at the
   Funeral of Henry D. Thoreau, of Concord, Massachusetts, Friday,
   May 9th, 1862."
        An 8 1/2" x 11" printed circular.

5 "The Funeral of Thoreau." Boston Transcript, 10 May.
        Reports on Thoreau's funeral. Reprinted in ESQ, no. 2
(1st Quarter 1965), pp. 16-17.

6 Obituary. New-York Daily Tribune, 10 May, p. 3.
        Reports on Thoreau's passing and notes his works and the local
regret. "He met death as gaily as Theramenses in Xenophon's story."
Reprinted in Glick, 1969, p. 13.

7 Report of Thoreau's funeral. Unidentified paper in the Harvard
   University Archives, 10 May.
        Describes the scene while the church bell tolled forty-four
times. William Ellery Channing's stanzas were song, the minister read
from the Bible, Emerson gave his address, Bronson Alcott read passages
from Thoreau's writings, and the Rev. Reynolds closed the service with
a prayer.

8 [SANBORN, FRANKLIN BENJAMIN.] "Thoreau." Concord Monitor, 10
   May, p. 28.

A sonnet honoring Thoreau. Corrected and reprinted:
1862.17.

9   [BARTLETT, S. RIPLEY.] "Walden." Concord Monitor, 17 May, pp.
     33–34.
          Verse.

10 "Deaths." Christian Register, 17 May.
          Paragraph on Thoreau reporting that "his decease
was consumption, and his last hours were among the calmest of his life.
Thus has passed away one of the most original thinkers our country has
produced." Reprinted in TSB, no. 109 (Fall 1969), p. 9.

11 "Personal Gossip; Literary, Political, and Miscellaneous." New
     York Leader, 17 May, p. 6.
          Notes Thoreau's funeral and reprints part of the Boston
Transcript notice of 10 May. Reprinted in Cameron, 1981b, p. 46.

12 "Walden." Concord Monitor, 17 May, p. 33–34.
          Comments on Thoreau's Walden hut saying: "This house is gone
long ago; but still by the shore he loved, one that is true and pure
enough can take warm hands and feel the throb of the faithful heart of
Henry D. Thoreau." Reprinted in ESQ, no. 7 (2d Quarter 1957), pp. 42–
43.

13 JACKSON, Dr. C.T. "Notice of the Death of Mr. Thoreau."
     Proceedings of the Boston Society of Natural History 9 (21
     May):70–72.
          A eulogy read before the Society that extols Thoreau's love
of nature. A resolution was passed expressing the Society's regret at
his death and mandating that a copy of this resolution be sent to his
mother and sister. Reprinted in TSB, no. 17 (October 1946), pp. 2–3.

14 R[ICKETSON], D[ANIEL]. "Walden." Liberator, 23 May, p. 84.
          Verse. Reprinted in Cameron, 1981b, pp. 46–47.

15 S[ANBORN], F[RANKLIN] B[ENJAMIN]. Liberator, 23 May, p. 84.
          The corrected version of sonnet noted in 1862.4. Reprinted in
Cameron, 1981b, p. 47.

16 "Personal Items." Herald of Progress 3 (24 May).
          Reports: "HENRY D. THOREAU, the student of Nature, and a
genial writer, died at Concord, N.H. [sic] on Tuesday May 6, after an
illness of eighteen months. His disease was consumption. 'His humor
and cheerful courage,' says the Tribune, 'did not forsake him during
his sickness and he met death as gaily as Theramenses in Xenophon's
story'" (see 1862.6).

1862

17 [SANBORN, FRANKLIN BENJAMIN.] "Thoreau." Concord Monitor, 24
      May, p. 24.
          Reprints a corrected version of the sonnet in 1862.8, noting
that it was first incorrectly published because it was not possible to
send the proof to the author. Reprinted in ESQ, no. 7 (2d Quarter
1957), p. 42.

18 "New publications." New-York Daily Tribune, 28 May, p. 2.
          Reviews the Thoreau article, "Walking," in the June Atlantic
Monthly, saying that "the quaint characteristic essay [is] . . . by the
late Henry Thoreau, whose recent decease imports an additional interest
to every production of his unique pen."

19 [HIGGINSON, STORROW.] "Henry D. Thoreau." Harvard Magazine 8
      (May):313-18.
          Describes the Thoreau that he used to see while going to
school in Concord in 1857. As he grew to know him he found him to be
"one of the rarest companions, beneath whose rugged exterior there lay
a lively appreciation of all that is vivifying in nature, and a natural
yearning towards his fellow-men, together with a kindly sympathy, which
was but the basis for his simple philosophy."

20 Review of the second printing of Walden. Concord Monitor, 7
      June, p. 53.
          "Walden is a book for boys and girls, for men and women, for
it is written by a man of heart, mind, and soul. . . . Read it again
and again . . . and you will surely find the sweet kernel of beauty,
knowledge, and truth." Reprinted in TSB, no. 129 (Fall 1974), p. 8.

21 PALMER, JOSEPH. Boston Daily Advertiser, 15 July, p. 3.
          A genealogical sketch mentioning that Thoreau's father was the
son of John and Jennie (Burns) Thoreau. His grandfather came from the
Island of Jersey. His grandmother's family were from Sterling,
Scotland. Gives a biographical sketch of Thoreau's life, noting that
he "led the life of a philosopher, subordinating all other pursuits and
so-called duties to his pursuit of knowledge, and to his own estimate
of duty. He was a man of firm mind and direct dealing; never discon-
certed, and not to be turned, by any inducement, from his own course.
He had a penetrating insight into men with whom he conversed, and was
not to be deceived or used by any party, and did not conceal his
disgust at any duplicity." Reprint: 1864.19.

22 [CURTIS, GEORGE WILLIAM.] "Editor's Easy Chair." Harper's
      Monthly Magazine 25 (July):270-71.
          A eulogy touching on Thoreau's schooling, philosophy, with
quotations from his books. "He was a man of singular rectitude,
independence, and sagacity." Reprinted in Glick, 1969, pp. 14-17.

23 BENTON, MYRON. "Thoreau's Writings." New York Leader, 16
      August, p. 1.
          A critical analysis of some of Thoreau's writing; with samples
of poetry. "Thoreau's style would be a model, were it not that a good
style is never modeled." Benton includes one of his own poems on
Thoreau. Facsimile printing in Cameron, 1977, pp. 40-42.

24 [EMERSON, RALPH WALDO.] "Thoreau." Atlantic Monthly 10
      (August):239-49.
          Prints a modified version of the speech given by Emerson at
Thoreau's funeral. Reprinted in Glick, 1969, pp. 18-19.

25 "New Publications." New-York Daily Tribune, 21 October, p. 6.
      Reports that Thoreau's essay "Wild Apples" will appear in the
November Atlantic Monthly.

                              1863

1 "The Works of Henry D. Thoreau." Boston Commonwealth, 13 March,
      p. 1.
          Gives a checklist of the Thoreau articles and poems published
in newspapers and magazines.

2 WASSON, D[AVID] A[TWOOD]. "Thoreau." Boston Commonwealth, 17
      April, p. [1]
          Verse. Reprinted in TSB, no. 123 (Spring 1973), pp. 3-4.

3 DORGAN, JOHN. "Walden." Boston Commonwealth, 25 September, p.
      1.
          Verse.

4 ALCOTT, LOUISA MAY. "Thoreau's Flute." Atlantic Monthly 12
      (September):280-82.
          Verse. Reprinted as Thoreau's Flute (Detroit: Edwin B.
Hill, 1899).

5 Review of Excursions. Boston Commonwealth, 23 October, p. 1.
          Lengthy review with many quotations from the book. Finds it
agreeable reading. "This book alone is enough to make memorable the
publishing harvest home of Messrs. Ticknor and Fields. It is the ripe
fruit of serious thought." Although some critics may claim that
Thoreau imitates Emerson as they used to say that Emerson copied
Carlyle, he is so full of his genius and himself that he could not be
an imitator of anyone.

6 "Thoreau's Excursions." New-York Daily Tribune, 31 October, p. 3.
          Quotes many passages from the book, ending with: "the volume

1863

abounds with delicious passages like the foregoing, full of strength
and sweetness of nature in her favorite dwelling places, and inspiring
admiration of the genius of the writer is spite of his apparent
churlishness toward his fellow-men, and his ungracious isolation from
living interests of society." Reprinted in Cameron, 1977, p. 42.

7 Review of Excursions. New-York Times, 23 November, p. 2.
       Notes that in the essays Thoreau shows that "civilized man to
him was nothing. Nature, all in all." While one Thoreau may be
admirable to tell the world some truths, a nation of them would be a
return to Indian life. The essays gathered here have much interest and
show "that he writes like a gentleman and a student familiar with the
current train of literature illustrative of the natural sciences, as
well as the common places of poetical allusion."

8 "Excursions of H.D. Thoreau." Essex (Mass.) Statesman, 28
      November.
       Disagrees with Thoreau's philosophy: "We do not believe that
God designed that one should be such a recluse as he was." Reprinted
in ATQ 14 (1972):112.

9 "Excursions." Arthur's Home Magazine 23 (November):62.
       "In personal and peculiarities and mental idiosycrancies, Mr.
Thoreau stands alone. We know of no better way of presenting him than
as a cultivated Indian."

10 CHANNING, WILLIAM ELLERY. "Henry David Thoreau." Boston
      Commonwealth, 25 December, p. 1.
       Prints Channing's reminiscences from his forthcoming book on
Thoreau.

11 Review of Excursions. Continental Monthly 4 (December):708-9.
       Comments that Thoreau's books "are in themselves a library for
the country, and we heartily commend them to all who love nature and
the fresh breath of the forest."

12 S[EARS], [EDMUND H.] Review of Excursions. Monthly Religious
      Magazine 30 (December):346-47.
       Commends the book to nature lovers who would like to see her
"through the eyes of one specially anointed as her priest and prophet."

13 "Excursions." Independent 15 (1863):783.
       The reviewer does not care for the book or for Thoreau,
calling him "a disgreeable man," but thinks "that his attempts to be a
barbarian were wise." Admits, however, that he knew nature and was a
master of good English. Thinks that "Mr. Emerson's introduction
overvalues Mr. Thoreau, and for this Mr. Emerson may be honored. He is
known to be generous of praise." Reprinted in ATQ, no. 2 (2d Quarter
1969), p. 31.

14 Proceedings of the Boston Society of Natural History 9 (1862–
    1863):70–71, 152.
        C.T. Jackson remarks on Thoreau's death and lists his
donations to the Society. Reports that on 21 May 1862 the Society
received a bequest of nearly one thousand species of New England
plants, also plants from Minnesota, New England birds' nests and eggs
and Indian antiquities. Reprinted in TSB, no. 73 (Fall 1960), p. 5.

15 Unidentified clipping pasted in Bronson Alcott's journal.
        A tribute from an unexpected source--Hon. Daniel Shattuck, the
local banker, who wrote that "Mr. Thoreau was a man who never conformed
his opinions after the model of others; they were his own; were also
singular. Who will say they were not right?"

16 "American Obituaries." In The National Almanac for 1863.
    Philadelphia: George W. Childs, p. 640.
        One-paragraph obituary on Thoreau saying that he had
"acquired considerable fame as an eccentric philosopher."

                              1864

1 CHANNING, WILLIAM ELLERY. "Reminiscences of Henry D. Thoreau."
   In six installments in Boston Commonwealth, 1 January, p. 1; 22
   January, p. 1; 29 January, p. 1; 5 February, p. 1; 12 February,
   p. 1; 19 February, p. 1.
       Prints freely edited extracts from Thoreau's journals that
are taken from Channing's as yet unpublished biography of Thoreau (see
1873.12).

2 "Henry D. Thoreau." Moore's Rural New Yorker, 16 January, p. 24.
       Speculates on the reason Thoreau remained an enigma to
everyone, including those who knew him best. Decides that the answer
must be in his words: "I long ago lost a hound, a bay horse, and a
turtle-dove and am still on their trail." States that the meaning of
these words will never be discovered nor will anyone ever know how much
the events or happenings referred to changed his subsequent life. Says
that his writings "have a singular fascination for all of those whose
hearts have anything in common with him, and who can look with charity
and patience upon his peculiar traits." Reprinted in Cameron, 1980b,
pp. 42–43.

3 "Walden." Circular, 28 March.
       Oneida Community weekly newpaper regrets that ten years
before, Walden was not noted by this paper because of "unappreciative,
if not thoroughly hostile reviews, together with a strong suspicion on
our part, of its egotism and eccentricity, it failed to get our
notice." Decides that the book is the "most original, sincere, and

1864

unaffected book that has recently been issued from the press."
Facsimile reprint in TSB, no. 115 (Spring 1971), p. 3.

4 "Another Book by Thoreau." Circular, 25 April.
     Oneida Community weekly newspaper finds much agreeable matter
in A Week on the Concord and Merrimack Rivers. Appreciates his
"quaint, subtle humor" and his knowledge of nature's ways but feels
that there is something lacking in his knowledge of man's spiritual
side. Does not agree with Thoreau's "glorification of Hindoo
philosophy; we cannot agree with his estimate of Christ." Gives some
extracts from the book. Facsimile reprint in TSB, no. 115 (Spring
1971), pp. 4-5.

5 J., S.H. "Thoughts at Oneida." Circular, 2 May.
     Oneida Community weekly newspaper comments on Thoreau's
philosophy regarding riches. His idea "was founded on the principle
that the smallest outlay that is essential to the necessary wants of
the mind and body, involves the least care."

6 Review of The Maine Woods. Round Table 1 (4 June):391.
     Notes that it consists of three Thoreau papers, two of which,
"Chesuncook" and "Khaadn," have been previously published. The third,
"The Allegash and East Branch," is printed for the first time. Feels
that not much of Thoreau's affection comes out in his writing, but the
little that does adds to his story. Enjoys the quiet humor. Thinks
that the detailed camping equipment will be of value to Maine visitors.
"The book will probably please such as are interested in the subject
which it treats. To our mind, however, there is too much attention
paid to insignificant details. What a traveler sees that is new or
important is one thing; what he does every minute is quite another.
Mr. Thoreau records both."

7 "The Maine Woods." New-York Times, 6 June, p. 2.
     Reviews The Maine Woods and finds that while there are some
objections to parts of it, there are acute observations and many
agreeable thoughts.

8 Review of The Maine Woods. Boston Commonwealth, 10 June, p. 1.
     Reprints long extracts from the book, with comments on each.
Says that some readers may find his prose dull but when they have
finished the book they will have an accurate picture of the area,
whereas some brightly written books leave no description of the region
when finished. Predicts that "Thoreau is a writer whose fame can only
grow by years."

9 "The Maine Woods." Circular, 27 June.
     Oneida Community weekly newpaper reviews The Maine Woods,
noting some readers may find the prose rather dull because it is what
Thoreau saw and heard, with no embellishment. As one follows the trip,

however, he will soon get a clear picture and "almost realize that he has felt the spray of water-falls upon his brow, that he has inhaled the odors of cedar and spruce and hemlock and forest shrubs."

10 "The Maine Woods." Eclectic Magazine 62 (July):379.
    Brief review calling it "just the book for the season for him who wants to get away from the haunts of men."

11 "Thoreau and The Maine Woods." New York Evening Post, 22 August,
    p. 1.
    Annotates long passages from the book with comments on Thoreau's keen qualities of observation and desire to learn more about nature, his wish to show things as they are. Reprinted in ATQ, no. 24 (Fall 1974), pp. 39-41.

12 [CONWAY, MONCURE D.] "The Transcendentalists of Concord."
    Fraser's Magazine 70 (August):245-64.
    Mainly about Emerson and his friends, with an occasional mention of Thoreau.

13 Review of The Maine Woods. Continental Monthly 6 (August):235-
    36.
    Favorable review calling it "truly original, natural, and American. Who among our descriptive writers can surpass H.D. Thoreau?"

14 [HIGGINSON, THOMAS WENTWORTH.] Review of The Maine Woods.
    Atlantic Monthly 14 (September):386-87.
    Admitting that Thoreau was a lover of nature, Higginson feels he has "an occasional mistiness of expression," and "an unnecessary defiance of tone and a very resolute non-appreciation of many things which a larger mental digestion can assimilate without discomfort." Reprinted in Glick, 1969, pp. 34-37.

15 "Book Notes, By a Parish Priest / Henry D. Thoreau." Church
    Monthly 7 (October):228-37.
    Reviews favorably A Week on the Concord and Merrimack Rivers and Walden, as well as the posthumous books, Excursions and The Maine Woods. The reviewer finds himself vicariously climbing Mount Katahdin and traveling miles in a Penobscot Indian canoe. Comments on the books, with quotations from them. Surprisingly, no lack of religious instincts is found. Discusses Thoreau's turn from organized religion, because he felt there were prejudices and bigotry, to a kind of pantheism, where he saw God in Nature. Thinks his writings will endure. Reprinted in Concord Saunterer, no. 2 (December 1985), pp. 49-55.

1864

16 "Review of The Maine Woods." Northern Monthly 1 (October):567.
Considers it "a book of uncommon worth; of straight-forward
earnestness and faithfulness. The descriptions, too, as so full of
life as to be pictures that stamp themselves into the memory, and stay
with you, like the balsam breathings of the woods you have passed
through." Recommends the book to people of Maine and to others who
wish to know the true Down-Easters.

17 "An American Rousseau." Saturday Review 18 (3 December):694-95.
Reviews Excursions with the comment "and now it is time to
speak of the volume lying before us, and we cannot do so but in terms
of very high admiration."

18 "The Maine Woods." Arthur's Home Magazine 25:95.
A brief mention of the book and its chapters.

19 PALMER, JOSEPH. Necrology of Alumni of Harvard College, 1851-52
to 1862-63. Boston: John Wilson & Son, pp. 430-32.
A genealogical and biographical sketch of Thoreau. "He led
the life of a philosopher, subordinating all other pursuits and so-
called duties to his pursuit of knowledge, and to his own estimate of
his duty." He is listed as he enrolled in college as David Henry
Thoreau. Notes that he spent six weeks in Canton boarding with Orestes
A. Brownson. Reprint of 1862.21.

1865

1 Review of Cape Cod. Boston Commonwealth, 25 March, p. 1.
Annotates extracts, concluding with: "So this
peripatetic philosopher jests, moralizes, sketches and chronicles; his
simple story, freighted with wit and wisdom, moving on to its too early
end; even as did the earthly life of him who told it." Facsimile
reprint in Cameron, 1973, pp. 158-59.

2 HIGGINSON, THOMAS WENTWORTH. Review of Cape Cod. Atlantic
Monthly 15 (March):381.
Admits some bareness in the book but states that Cape Cod
is that way also. Feels that Thoreau's one perfect poem, "My life is
like a stroll upon the beach," must have been inspired by such a
locality. Finds some inaccuracies, but says they are trivial. "Cape
Cod does not change its traits, only its boundaries, and this book will
stand for it, a century hence, as it now does." Reprinted in Harding,
1954, pp. 41-43.

3 Review of Cape Cod. Independent 17 (27 April):8.
Notes that Thoreau occasionally brings in extraneous material,
but in the main there is much entertaining writing and "his style is
properly English and of good order. His descriptions are graphic and

forcible. . . . [His] dry humor is forever breaking out and is rarely pushed to excess or becomes weak."

    4 Review of <u>Cape Cod</u>. <u>New-York Times</u>, 2 May, p. 2.
        One-paragraph review noting Thoreau's ability for keen observation and expressing pleasure that his friends are collecting and preserving his writings in this fashion.

    5 "<u>Cape Cod</u>." <u>Harper's Monthly</u> 30 (May):806.
        Advises the residents of the Cape that they "must not be offended if they and their dwelling place are treated as if they were curious specimens of antediluvian civilization. Thoreau treats his own Concord in the same passionless strain."

    6 S[EARS], [EDMUND H.]. Review of <u>Cape Cod</u>. <u>Monthly Religious Magazine</u> 33 (May):319–20.
        Finds the book entertaining even though the descriptions seem to be in "caricature."

    7 SORDELLO [pseud.]. "Thoreau and His Writings." <u>New York Evening Post</u>, 10 June, p. 1.
        Notes that the half-cultured readers who must have rhetoric will not find it in Thoreau's writings, for his are based on his experiences and are simple and natural. Nor is he for the voluptuary, the frivolous, or the pious. Reviews <u>Cape Cod</u> and believes that it "will always be a book of today. . . . His quality may be likened to that of a hickory stick––dry, clean, close, and of enduring virtue." Reprinted in Cameron, 1980a, pp. 43–44.

    8 Review of <u>Cape Cod</u>. <u>Peterson's Magazine</u> 47 (June):449.
        Brief paragraph saying: "We have always been charmed with Thoreau's books." He wrote with simplicity and accuracy.

    9 "Thoreau's Letters." <u>New-York Daily Tribune</u>, 20 July, p. 6.
        Writes that Thoreau's letters have some revelations into his original but not very deep mind and that they are always hard and cold, "often oracular in their tone." Comments that his poetry, published in the final pages, has "little beauty of imagery and no sweetness of expresssion."

   10 BABSON, EMMA MORTIMER. "Walden Pond." <u>Boston Commonwealth</u>, 22 July.
        Verse.

   11 Review of <u>Letters to Various Persons</u>. New York Times, 31 July, p. 5.
        Notes that Emerson was the editor but sees little of interest to anyone except those to whom the letters were addressed. The ills of

1865

the world cannot be solved by his "cold and selfish isolation from human cares and interests."

12 "Cape Cod." New Englander 24 (July):602-3.
      Says that the book "abounds in that interest which sharp observation, and minute and faithful recording, even of the most trivial objects, never fails to impart."

13 Review of Cape Cod. Universalist Quarterly 22 (July):399.
      Finds the book fresh and agreeable and "in full sympathy with Nature and all her moods."

14 WEISS, JOHN. "Thoreau." Christian Examiner 79 (July):96-117.
      A classmate writes that Thoreau was undistinguished in college and indifferent to gaining honors. No one suspected the fine genius in development. He loved old English literature and had a large library of it. Thoreau "passed for nothing, it is suspected, with most of us; for he was cold and unimpressionable. . . . He did not care for people; his classmates seemed very remote." He had not yet become a naturalist, and yet he seemed to be living alone on some Walden Pond part of his college years. He indulged in none of the college pranks. Had Thoreau been other than he was it might have weakened his genius. Reprinted in Harding, 1971, pp. 36-43.

15 "Literary Review / Letters." Boston Commonwealth, 12 August, p. 1.
      Complains about the sparseness of the letters. Many of the letters to his family are omitted because of personal reasons; several of his correspondents are entirely overlooked. Agrees, however, that it is "not possible that we shall ever find in so few pages so much of the genuine life and spirit of the man." Regrets that the book is not annotated and gives the life of Cholmondely to show how someone in the future should do this.

16 "Thoreau's Letters." New York Independent 17 (24 August):2.
      Gives many quotations from the letters to illustrate the type of person Thoreau was--not so much "gossipy as literary." "Seldom has a volume appeared more quotable. It is as full of meat as the nuts in the woods he loved and knew so well." Reprinted in Cameron, 1977, p. 46.

17 E[LLIS], [RUFUS]. Review of Letters to Various Persons. Monthly Religious Magazine 34 (September):191.
      Feels that Thoreau is too indifferent in his writings to the struggle between the states. Extracts from some of the letters are printed under "Random Readings."

18 "Letters to Various Persons." Radical 1 (September):32.
      Prints several extracts with comments.

19 "New Publications / Cape Cod." Catholic World 6 (September):283.
     Finds the book very readable with "keen observations, and
quaint remarks sprinkled all over its pages," but with occasional
skepticism. Believes that Thoreau was deeply religious but could not
relate his religious feelings to the denominations of his day. Quotes
an extract to show his talent for description.

20 New-York Daily Tribune, 26 October, p. 6.
     Reprints extracts from 1865.17, deciding that "Mr. Thoreau is
more happily delineated [than Mr. Emerson] by the critic, who appears
to have gained a true perspective of the Walden Pond philosopher, in
spite of the illusory veil, which his admirers have thrown around his
remains since his decease." Reprinted in Cameron, 1973, pp. 164–65.

21 [HIGGINSON, THOMAS WENTWORTH.] "Review of Letters to Various
     Persons." Atlantic Monthly 16 (October): 504–5.
     Sees in the letters the heart and soul of Thoreau and mostly
finds him an admirable person. Applauds his thoughts on love and
marriage and finds them unexpected in one of such an unsocial nature.

22 [LOWELL, JAMES RUSSELL.] "Thoreau." North American Review 101
     (October):597–608.
     While ostensibly a review of Letters to Various Persons, this
is an attack on Thoreau and his writings. The first few pages are
concerned with transcendentalism, then Lowell turns his attention to
Thoreau, who has such a high opinion of himself that he regards all of
his weakness and defects as virtues and powers. He had little active
imagination; of receptive he had much. His appreciation is of the
highest quality; his critical power, from want of continuity of mind,
very limited and inadequate. And thus for several pages he seeks to
destroy Thoreau. However, admits that Thoreau's prose is of the best
ever written. Reprint: part in 1871.2; in full: 1871.9; lacking the
transcendental introduction in Glick, 1969, pp. 38–46.

23 Review of A Week on the Concord and Merrimack Rivers, Walden,
     and The Maine Woods. Universalist Quarterly 22
     (October):530–31.
     Commends the books for bringing the reader closer to nature
but feels that on occasion some remarks are "shallow, egotistical, and
impertinent."

24 "Thoreau's Letters." New Englander 24 (October):805.
     Brief paragraph saying that there had been hopes that the
letters would shed some light on the secret of Thoreau's
idiosyncrasies, but they did not. There is, however, an occasional
passage that "reveals a capacity for tenderness and love which
surprises the reader almost to tears."

1865

25 BALL, B.W. "Old Concord--Sleepy Hollow Cemetery--Hawthorne--
    Thoreau." Boston Courier, 25 November, p. 4.
        Praises Thoreau's stand against materialism. Claims that he
has many readers and that sooner or later there will be beneficial
results to society because of his life and teachings. Reprinted in
Cameron, 1980b, pp. 100–101.

26 ADAMS, CHARLES H. "Thoreau." Yale Literary Magazine 31
    (November):57–66.
        Perceptive view of Thoreau, saying that if one carefully
reads his books he will look at the world with "wiser and more headful
eyes."

27 "Thoreau's Cape Cod." Unidentified source.
        Notes that most of the book is made up of essays previously
published in the Atlantic Monthly. While it is fresh and interesting
its humor is rarely droll, often grim and forced. The style of the
sketches is admirable, and the reader will almost smell the salt ocean
air. Reprinted in Cameron, 1973, p. 159.

28 ALCOTT, AMOS BRONSON. Emerson. Cambridge: Privately printed,
    p. 61.
        Mentions Thoreau.

29 ALCOTT, LOUISA MAY. Moods. Boston: Loring, 297 pp.
        A novel in which, some speculate, the character of Adam
Warwick is based on Thoreau because he is virtuous, devoted to nature,
and a scholar who adheres rigidly to his principles.

1866

1 COLBY, J.W. "Thoreau." Cambridge (Mass.) Chronicle, 31 March,
   pp. 1–2.
        Notes that while Thoreau lived he received little more fame than
that he wore his hair long and that he was graduated from Harvard. Now
there are "fashionable attentions" given to him, and his "rejected
manuscripts are being hunted up and printed." It is to be wondered
that so few recognized his worth while he was alive. He was not a
recluse, and while at Walden his door was open to all. The company of
some people was irksome to him, and he was impatient with common minds.
"Thoreau has been somewhat harshly dealt with by the critics, but it
will only give us another example of their maculateness and false
augury; and he will have tender remembrance in the hearts of uncounted
admirers, when their ephemeral brilliancy is extinct." Reprinted in
Cameron, 1977, p. 47.

2 [CONWAY, MONCURE DANIEL.] "Thoreau." <u>Fraser's Magazine</u> 73
(April):447–65.
     Carefully describes Thoreau's appearance as short, well-built,
with bright blue eyes and a strong aquiline-Roman nose that reminded
Conway of the prow of a ship. Gives a generally favorable appraisal of
Thoreau's character and his writings. Reprinted: 1866.3

3 [CONWAY, MONCURE DANIEL.] "Thoreau." <u>Every Saturday</u> 1 (16
June):662–64.
     Reprint of 1866.2.

4 [CONWAY, MONCURE DANIEL] "Thoreau." <u>National Anti-Slavery
Standard</u>, 23 June, p. 4.
     Reprint of 1866.2.

5 ALGER, W[ILLIAM] R[OUNSEVILLE]. "The Hermit of Concord."
<u>Monthly Religious Magazine</u> 35 (June):382–89.
     Critical study of Thoreau's aloofness. "Many a humble and
loving author, who has nestled amongst his fellow-men and not boasted,
has contributed far more to brace and enrich the characters, and
sweeten the lives of his readers, than the ill-balance and unsatisfied
hermit of Concord, part cynic, part stoic, who strove to compensate
himself with nature and solitude for what he could not wring from
society."

6 M'DUFFIE, JOHN. "In Memorium. Henry D. Thoreau, Concord, Mass.
/ Theodore Parker, Florence, Italy." <u>Cambridge</u> (Mass.)
<u>Chronicle</u>, 21 July, p. 4.
     A poem read at the Parker Pic Nic, at Walden Pond, 11
July, mourning the loss of these two men. Reprinted in Cameron, 1977,
49.

7 "The Parker-Fraternity Picnic." Unidentified newspaper.
     Reports on a picnic held on 11 July at Walden Pond at which an
original poem by John M'Duffie about Thoreau and the pond was read.

8 Report of the 10th annual picnic of the Parker Fraternity held a
Walden Pond on 11 July. <u>National Anti-Slavery Standard</u>, unknown
date.
     At the picnic several asked where Thoreau's hut was located
and at least one hundred visited this shrine, which was considered to
be a "curious specimen of the progress of hero-worship." Comments on
Thoreau's stay at Walden: "If an experiment, it was a successful one,
for Thoreau's abandonment of it after the first year showed that he had
learned (what other people knew before) that the civilized method of
habitation is more comfortable and satisfactory than the savage."
Reprinted in Cameron, 1973, p. 168.

1866

9 [CONWAY, MONCURE DANIEL] "Thoreau." Eclectic Magazine 67 (August):180–95.
Reprint of 1866.2.

10 Review of A Yankee in Canada. New York Times, 26 September, p. 2.
Brief review, saying "the account of the tour is not especially fresh or entertaining . . . the essays or addresses are full of doctrines which all but Radicals would not put down as heresies."

11 Review of A Yankee in Canada. Boston Commonwealth, 29 September, p. 4.
Notes that Thoreau found few readers when he was alive and even fewer who agreed with his philosophy, but since his death his true genius is becoming known and appreciated. Finds the arrangement of the essays confusing and suggests a better order. Likes the bits of humor in the book.

12 BENSON, EUGENE. "Literary Frondeurs." Galaxy 2 (September):78–82.
Explains that a frondeur in ancient armies was the one who was trained to use the sling. David was one. A literary frondeur is one who slings truths at shams or "mumbo-jumbo of society." Thoreau used his sling on cities, clergymen, newspapers and most of society. After explaining his terms he gives a rebuttal to Lowell's article (see 1865.22). Reprinted in TSB, no. 32 (July), pp. 3–4.

13 "Thoreau's A Yankee in Canada / A Characteristic Book--The Humors of Travel." New York Evening Post, 4 October, p. 1.
Considers Thoreau one of his generation who has escaped from the bonds of conventionality and actually lived his own life. Long excerpts are quoted.

14 "Book Table / A Yankee in Canada; with Anti-Slavery Papers." New York Evening Post, 11 October, pp. 2–3.
Records for the first time Thoreau's well-known diary comment on the return to him of the unsold copies of his first book, A Week on the Concord and Merrimack Rivers, which reads: "I have now a library of some nine hundred volumes--seven hundred of which I wrote myself." Briefly reviews the essays in the book.

15 "New Publications / A Yankee in Canada." New-York Daily Tribune, 25 October, p. 6.
A long review in which Thoreau's Maine trip is carefully covered as well as his other books stating that "every succeeding book of Thoreau makes him more truly loved and leaned upon."

16 CONWAY, MONCURE D[ANIEL]. "Walt Whitman." Fortnightly Review 6 (October):538–48.

Calls Thoreau a <u>Yogi</u> who spent his life in the woods studying the Puranas and the Baghavat Geeta. Notes that he who has almost no reputation abroad will be remembered with the best thinkers and scholars who ever lived in America. Thoreau met Whitman in 1856; his <u>Letters to Various Persons</u> contains two letters to the poet telling him about Oriental books and other information. Quotes part of another Thoreau letter to a friend telling him about Whitman.

17   Review of <u>A Yankee in Canada</u>. <u>Universalist Quarterly</u> 23 (October):513.
     Briefly recommends the book.

18   E[LLIS], [RUFUS]. Review of <u>A Yankee in Canada</u>. <u>Monthly Religious Magazine</u> 36 (November):334–39.
     Commends the book as "pleasant and not uninstructive and always high-toned."

19   "<u>A Yankee in Canada</u>." <u>Eclectic Magazine</u> 67 (November):636.
     Brief review closing with: "His asceticism tinged his mind and made him morbid on many subjects."

20   ALGER, WILLIAM ROUNSEVILLE. "Thoreau." In <u>The Solitudes of Nature and Man</u>. Boston: Roberts Brothers, pp. 329–38.
     The author repeats Lowell's indictment of Thoreau as one who had and desired only weak alliances with mankind. Many authors who have lived among their fellowmen and not boasted about it have enriched their readers much more than "the ill-balanced and unsatisfied hermit of Concord." The writer, however, does admit that he has had pleasure in reading Thoreau and that "his interior life, with relations of thoughts and things, was intensely tender and true, however sorely ajar he may have been with persons and with ideas of persons." Reprinted as "Apostle of Solitude" in Harding, 1971, pp. 44–53.

1867

1   "New England / Clark's Island / A Trace of Thoreau." <u>New-York Daily Tribune</u>, 31 August.
    Describes a Thoreau misjudgement at Clarks' Island: "One day Thoreau himself, a short, broad, awkward man, much in feature, I am told, like Mr. Emerson—burst in upon his island friends. He had attempted to walk across the harbor bed between here and Duxbury, but, within a hundred feet of land and to call out for a dory. For once, the great, wise walker miscalculated his travel." Reprinted in Cameron, 1973, p. 182.

2   "Autumn Tints." <u>New Dominion Monthly</u> 1 (October):14–16.
    Early reprinting of this Thoreau essay in a country outside the United States.

1867

3 Fitchburg (Mass.) Sentinal, 22 November.
    One-paragraph partial breakdown of a year of Thoreau's
expenses while at Walden.

4 Fitchburg (Mass.) Sentinal, 24 November.
    Further breakdown into individual items of Thoreau's expenses
    noted in 1867.3

5 [SANBORN, FRANKLIN BENJAMIN.] Review of A Week on the Concord
    and Merrimack Rivers. Boston Commonwelth, 21 December, p. 16.
    Writing of the new edition, Sanborn states that there is still
a demand for a book that did not sell twenty years before. Describes
the book as one that will live beyond the present books. "To the
hearty admirers of Henry Thoreau his first book will always seem his
best."

1868

1 "Literature." Putnam's Magazine 1 (February):257.
    Brief comment on the new and revised edition of A Week on the
Concord and Merrimack Rivers, noting that twenty years earlier Thoreau
had uphill work getting public acceptance. Believes that his writings
have excellent qualities.

2 "An Hour with a Philosopher / Alcott's Opinion on Emerson,
    Thoreau and His Style of Life." New-York Daily Tribune, 12
    August, p. 2.
    A young man reports on his interview with Alcott and the
responses to his questions about Thoreau. Was told that Thoreau went
to Walden just to get a taste of the savage life. He was friendly with
those who were in agreement with him and did not go out of his way to
visit anyone. Facsimile printing in Cameron, 1973, pp. 192-94.

3 LANG, THOMAS. "Walden Pond." Unidentified source.
    Notes that the traveler from Boston on the Fitchburg Railroad
may have noticed a small pond near Concord. Lang investigated the pond
and says that Walden pointed out the beauty of the pond and that the
opening of the railroad made it more accessible. Reprinted in Cameron,
1973, pp. 187-88.

4 HAWTHORNE, NATHANIEL. Passages from the American Note-Books.
    Vol. 2. Boston: Ticknor & Fields, pp. 96-99.
    On 1 and 2 September 1842, Hawthorne writes of his talks with
Thoreau about Indians and his purchase of the book that the brothers
used for their trip related in A Week on the Concord and Merrimack
Rivers. Notes that Thoreau instructed him in the use of the boat.

1869

1   [CURTIS, GEORGE WILLIAM.] "Editor's Chair." Harper's Monthly
     Magazine 38 (February):415-16.
         Describes a visit with Thoreau and a discussion of American
Indians. The article then turns to a discussion of Daniel Boone,
Cromwell, Lady Cavaliere, the Norman Conquest, and even Columbus.

2   [ALCOTT, LOUISA MAY.] "Merry's Monthly Chat with Her Friends."
     Merry's Museum, March, p. 147.
         Miss Alcott tells of Thoreau's announcements of the arrival of
spring. Facsimile printing in TSB, no. 18 (January), p. 1.

3   MUNROE, ALFRED. "Concord / Thoreau's Successor / The New Hermit
     of Walden Pond." New-York Times, 24 April, p. 2.
         Account of a visit to a young man [Edmond S. Hotham] living a
Thoreau-like life at Walden Pond. Notes that Thoreau's grave, having
been removed from its original resting place, is now at Sleepy Hollow
Cemetery across from Hawthorne's.

4   [SANBORN, FRANKLIN BENJAMIN.] "Thoreau's Love of Music / His
     favorite Songs." Springfield Republican, 23 June, p. 2.
         Thoreau liked certain forms of music. His favorite songs were
Mrs. Hemans's "Pilgrim Fathers"; Moore's "Evening Bells"; "Canadian
Song"; Wolfe's "Burial of Sir John Moore"; and "Tom Bowlin." He played
the flute with much sweetness. Reprinted in Cameron, 1981a, p. 7.

5   "Cape Cod: Henry D. Thoreau." New-York Daily Tribune, 24 July,
     p. 5.
         Reminiscences of a man who met Thoreau in 1850 at Highland
Light, Cape Cod. Describes in detail a walk with him and their
discovery of arrowheads and various plants. Reprinted in ATQ, no. 14,
pt. 3, (Spring 1972), pp. 123-24.

6   [CHANNING, WILLIAM ELLERY.] "Henry Thoreau / A Faithful
     Portraiture." Unidentified source.
         Selections from Channing's forthcoming book describing Thoreau
as he knew him. Reprinted in Cameron, 1973, p. 221.

7   [CHANNING, WILLIAM ELLERY.] "Thoreau's Travels / Where He Went
     and What He Did There." Unidentified source.
         More selections from Channing's forthcoming book on Thoreau,
relating information on Thoreau's preparations for his various trips.
Reprinted in Cameron, 1973, p. 224.

8   RICKETSON, DANIEL. The Autumn Sheaf. New Bedford: D.
     Ricketson, pp. 198, 199, 209.
         Prints three Ricketson poems about Thoreau, "Walden," "In

1869

Memorium: To H.D.T.," and "The Improved Dance." Reprinted in
Ricketson, Daniel Ricketson and His Friends, ed. Anna and Walton
Ricketson (Boston: Houghton, Mifflin, 1902), pp. 19, 152, 322. "The
Improved Dance" is renamed "Thoreau's Dance."

1870

1 "A Visit to Old Concord." Unidentified source, August.
      Gives an itinerary for a walk to the main attractions in
Concord, including Walden Pond. Notes that Thoreau's hut was removed
to the north of the village to be used as a corn-crib and finally
demolished. Believes that Thoreau would be happy that "such secondary
traces of him are gone." Thoreau's appearance is described, as well
his nature and philosophy. He was "perhaps the richest character that
ever lived in Concord." Reprinted in Cameron, 1973, p. 235.

2 "A. Bronson Alcott on the Authors of New England." Unidentifed
      source.
      Alcott in his address refers to Thoreau as one who decided
that the "best thing any young man could do to prove he could survive
and feed his genius on books, would be to leave civilized society since
there were so many hinderances in civilization." And he took his own
advice and went to live at Walden Pond. Reprinted in Cameron, 1973,
p. 231.

3 "Of New England Authors." Unidentified St. Louis newspaper.
      Review of Alcott's St. Louis address in which he includes a
sketch of Thoreau and his attitude towards government and liberty.
Describes Thoreau's feelings about his release from jail before paying
his tax. Reprinted in Cameron, 1973, p. 236.

4 GRISWOLD, RUFUS WILMOT. The Prose Writers of America.
      Philadelphia: Porter & Coates, pp. 657-59.
      Prefaces selections from Thoreau's works with a biographical
sketch noting that while he lived on a small amount of money while at
Walden, the quality of his life was also sparse. Such a life would not
be tempting to anyone. "Thoreau, a man of humors, led a dreamy,
meditative, philosophic sort of life, apparently without any definite
aim."

5 Peabody Museum of American Archaeology and Ethnology. Third
      Annual Report. Boston: Press of A.A. Kingman, pp. 6-7.
      Notes that Thoreau's Indian artifacts collection was presented
to the museum by Thoreau's estate.

1871

1 "Concord in Winter." Springfield Republican, 20 January, p. 6.
   A Cincinnati visitor to Concord recounts his visit to the homes and graves of Hawthorne and Thoreau and the talk he had at the cemetery with one who had planted trees at the pond with Thoreau. Called Thoreau "an odd man." Reprinted in TSB, no. 136 (Summer 1976), pp. 6–8.

2 "Thoreau." Every Saturday 10 (18 February):166.
   Selections on Thoreau taken from Lowell's My Study Windows (see 1865.22).

3 "Fuller, Thoreau, Emerson." Boston Commonwealth, 6 May, pp. 1–2.
   Reports on an Alcott lecture similar to his other author talks.

4 "A. Bronson Alcott / Lecture on New England Authors."
   Unidentified newpaper clipping.
   Mentions many of Thoreau's peculiarities but calls him a genius and says that there never will be another like him. "One is enough." Reprinted in Cameron, 1973, p. 242.

5 "A Colloquial Poem / Mr. Channing's 'Wanderer.'" Unidentified source.
   Notes that Channing's earlier books of poems are now out of print and were harshly treated when published. Several of the poems about Thoreau are reprinted.

6 "New England Authors." Unidentified source.
   In a lecture at Chicago, Alcott summarizes in one paragraph the life that Thoreau led at Walden Pond. Reprinted in Cameron, 1973, p. 242.

7 ALLIBONE, S. AUSTIN. A Critical Dictionary of English Literature. Vol. 3. Philadelphia: J.B. Lippincott, pp. 2406–7.
   Brief biographical sketch.

8 CHANNING, WILLIAM ELLERY. The Wanderer: A Short Colloquial Poem. Boston: James R. Osgood & Co., pp. 25–37, 47–48, 56, 61–74.
   Refers poetically to Thoreau. Calls him "Eidolon." The final pages above relate a poem entitled "Henry's Camp" telling of a camping trip to Wachusett with him.

9 LOWELL, JAMES RUSSELL. "Thoreau." In My Study Windows. Boston: James R. Osgood, pp. 193–209.
   Reprint of 1865.22. Also reprinted, less the transcendental introductory, in Glick, 1969, pp. 38–46.

1872

1 "The Mother of Thoreau." <u>Salem</u> (Mass.) <u>Observer</u>, 6 April, p. 1.
    Notice of the death of Thoreau's mother who was "a woman of
more than common powers of mind,--witty, resolute and vivacious, warmly
attached to her family and friends, and to the causes she espoused."
Reprinted in Cameron, 1980b, p. 48.

2 A Preview of Alcott's <u>Concord Days</u>." <u>Springfield Republican</u>, 21
    May, pp. 5-6.
    Summarizes the section on Thoreau's ancestry from Alcott's
soon-to-be published book. Reprinted in Cameron, 1981a, p. 13.

3 RICKETSON, DANIEL. "Thoreau's Cairn." Unidentified source,
    12 August.
    Prints a poem about a visit to the cairn with Alcott.
Reprinted in Cameron, 1973, p. 262.

4 "Nathaniel Hawthorne." <u>Harper's Monthly Magazine</u> 45 (October):
    688 and passim.
    Shows a sketch of the gravestones of Thoreau and Hawthorne.

5 [SANBORN, FRANKLIN BENJAMIN.] "Wilson Flagg's Woods and By-
    Ways." <u>Springfield Republican</u>, 13 December, pp. 5-6.
    Compares Flagg's prose with Thoreau's and finds that the
former's writings are "peculiar and attractive, not stimulating, as
Thoreau's ideas are, but soothing and calmly suggestive, like the
influences of a light twilight no longer enflamed by the glories of the
sunset." Reprinted in Cameron, 1981a, pp. 17-18.

6 ALCOTT, A[MOS] BRONSON. "Thoreau." In <u>Concord Days</u>. Boston:
    Roberts Brothers, pp. 11-20.
    Finds Thoreau an excellent companion for walking and
talking, perhaps a bit over-confident by genius and too stiffly an
individual at times. He possessed the Spartan and Stoic virtues.
Added to the chapter is biography of Thoreau by Channing.

7 FLAGG, WILSON. "Thoreau." In <u>The Woods and By-Ways of New
    England</u>. Boston: James R. Osgood, pp. 392-96.
    Believes Thoreau went to the woods to see if it were possible
for men who had obtained the knowledge of civilization to retain the
simplicity of early society. He hoped to prove what Rousseau described
but did not have the willpower to live. He was a poet more than a
philosopher. Notes that only an excavation marks the spot of Thoreau's
hut. "It has not yet been desecrated by a monument such as men erect
to those who have flattered their prejudices and exalted their pride,
the proud distinction of worldlings after their death." Reprinted:
1881.18.

8 HART, JOHN H. "Henry D. Thoreau." In A Manual of American
    Literature. Philadelphia: Eldredge & Bro., p. 477.
        Short sketch calling Thoreau a complete humorist "in the old
English sense of a man who indulges in humor."

9 UNDERWOOD, FRANCIS H. "Henry David Thoreau." In A Handbook
    of English Literature: American Authors. Boston: Lee, pp. 114–
17.
        Brief biographical sketch with extracts from Thoreau's
writings.

1873

1 [SANBORN, FRANKLIN BENJAMIN.] "Channing's Thoreau: Poet-
    Naturalist." Springfield Republican, 5 March, pp. 5–6.
        Previews Channing's life of Thoreau, noting the closeness
of the two men. Notes that Thoreau's sister, Sophia, is about to sell
his home of the last twelve years of his life. It is hoped that it
will fall into the hands of one who will value its associations.
Reprinted in Cameron, 1981a, pp. 19–20.

2 [SANBORN, FRANKLIN BENJAMIN.] "Thoughts on Cape Cod."
    Springfield Republican, 24 July, p. 5.
        Notes that though the Cape has changed since Thoreau's day,
after twenty years his is still the best guidebook to the region.
Reprinted in Cameron, 1981a, pp. 21–22.

3 [SANBORN, FRANKLIN BENJAMIN.] "Thoreau, Channing, and the
    Wayside Inn at Sudbury." Springfield Republican, 4 September, p.
    8.
        Quotes from Channing's "Walks and Talks" chapter from his life
of Thoreau, being published that week by Roberts. This extract
describes the Wayside Inn. Reprinted in Cameron, 1981a, p. 222.

4 [SANBORN, FRANKLIN BENJAMIN.] "Higginson's Oldport Days / How He
    Compares with Hawthorne, Emerson and Thoreau / The Excellent
    Crayon Portrait of Thoreau in Channing's New Book." Springfield
    Republican, 15 September, pp. 4–5.
        The writings of many authors do not achieve great popularity
in their own time, and this book may take its place with those of
Hawthorne, Emerson, and Thoreau in that respect. Compares Higginson
and Thoreau as students of nature. Notes that two-thirds of the 1,500-
copy edition of Channing's life of Thoreau has been sold in less than a
fortnight. Reprinted Cameron, 1981a, p. 23.

5 Review of Channing's Thoreau: The Poet-Naturalist. Worcester
    (Mass.) Spy, 16 September.
        Finds the book an agreeable study of Thoreau.

1873

6 "Thoreau: The Poet-Naturalist. With Memorial Verses. By
   William Ellery Channing." New-York Weekly Tribune, 17 September.
        Thoreau could not have been born in any other place or time
and been what he was. New England was in a period of "effervescence"
and helped produce a Thoreau. Channing's book is "colored with the
soft prismatic light of personal affection." Describes Thoreau's
background, habits, likes, and aversions as well as his physical
appearance. Facsimile printing in Cameron, 1973a, pp. 269-71.

7 Review of Thoreau: The Poet-Naturalist. Boston Transcript, 7
   October, p. 6.
        Considers the book "readable as much for its quaint biographer
as for its curious bits of biography."

8 Review of Thoreau: The Poet-Naturalist. Monthly Religious
   Magazine 50 (October):383-84.
        Gives a "vivid and, we doubt not, a true picture of
his mind and character, which was marked by the inconsistencies which
belong to a person who is at the same time genuine and sincerely
affected."

9 Review of Thoreau: The Poet-Naturalist. New Englander 125
   (October):765-66.
        Complains of "Mr. Channing's astonishing and marvelous
acrobatic word flights" and is looking to learn something about Thoreau
but finding nothing much but Channing. Hopes that some time there will
be a biography in which Thoreau will be completely portrayed and
criticized.

10 Review of Thoreau: the Poet-Naturalist. Christian Register, 8
    November.
        Condemns the book: "Mr. Channing has a 'damnable iteration,'
a most insufferable style, a poor sort of wit, and a general crabbed-
ness."

11 BROWN, WILLIAM HAND. Review of Thoreau: The Poet-Naturalist.
    Southern Magazine 13 (November):628-32.
        Desires not what Channing has given in this book but some real
insight into Thoreau's character, not as an admirable person, not as an
influence in his generation, but merely as an "amiable oddity."
Thoreau seemed to lack coordination of his faculties.

12 CHANNING, WILLIAM ELLERY. Thoreau: The Poet-Naturalist. Boston:
    Roberts Brothers, 357 pp.
        In this first attempt at a full-length biography of Thoreau,
the author, who knew him better than anyone else, gives many
interesting anecdotes intermixed with much extraneous matter that has
little place in this biography and only serves to confuse the reader.
Such are the two chapters, "Walks and Talks" and "Walks and Talks

Continued," which were added at the last moment "to furnish a more
familiar idea of Thoreau's walks with his friends." The approach to
Thoreau's life is not objective but rather that of a close friend who
is endeavoring to give Thoreau some measure of immortality. Gives many
of Thoreau's previously unpublished quotations but does not identify
them. The book concludes with eight memorial verses. Six sections of
the book were published in Boston Commonwealth (see 1864.1).

1874

1   "Mr William Ellery Channing's Thoreau." Nation 18 (8 January):
    29–30.
        Reports negatively on both Thoreau and his biographer.
Channing "was the most self-willed and conceited of the Orphic School,"
while Thoreau "has shown himself to be the most wilful."

2   "A Talk with Emerson / His Views on Prominent Literary
    Characters." Chicago Daily Tribune (supplement), 10 January.
        Calls Thoreau a true genius who "would need another Linnaeus,
as well as a poet, properly to edit his writings." Reprinted in
Cameron, 1977, p. 65.

3   [JAPP, ALEXANDER HAY.] "Henry Thoreau, The Poet-Naturalist."
    British Quarterly 59 (January):181–94.
        The book is agreeable, and, in spite of Thoreau's roughness,
his character is pure and sweet. Finds in Thoreau "a fiery hatred of
wrong," one of the main ingredients of heroism. Reprinted in 1874.6.

4   "Concord Authors." Boston Daily Globe, February.
        Review of an Alcott lecture before the Historic-Genealogical
Society, in which he again notes that Thoreau was one of a kind, and
that there will never be another like him. Reprinted in Cameron, 1973,
pp. 276–77.

5   [SANBORN, FRANKLIN BENJAMIN.] "Recent Literature." Atlantic
    Monthly 33 (February):230–31.
        Reviews Thoreau: The Poet-Naturalist. Believes that while
Channing's "rhetoric and syntax are eccentric," and he "occasionally
becomes tiresome," it does give a better picture than ever before of
Thoreau's complex nature, which has not previously been understood
either by his admirers or those who did not care for him.

6   [JAPP, ALEXANDER HAY.] "Henry David Thoreau, The Poet-
    Naturalist." Littell's Living Age, 14 March, pp. 543–50.
        Credits the book to Dr. W.D. Channing and gives the date of
Thoreau's death as 8 May instead of 6 May. Reprint of 1874.3.

1874

7   A., R.E. "A Summer Ramble to the Hermit-House of Thoreau."
    Boston Journal, 3 July.
        A visitor to the site of Thoreau's hut describes the scene in
1874, noting that at one end of the pond there is now a building for
the convenience of picnic parties.

8   WISWELL, E.R. "Thoreau's Unpublished Works." New-York Weekly
    Tribune, 8 July.
        Writes of a visit with Thoreau's mother and sister, who showed
him thirteen volumes of his journal; notes that there is enough
material for several more books. He does not feel that "the thoughts
and observations of such a rare thinker and observer as Thoreau" should
be concealed. Facsimile printing in Cameron, 1973, pp. 271–72.

9   [CURTIS, GEORGE WILLIAM.] "Editor's Easy Chair." Harper's
    Monthly Magazine 34 (July):284.
        Curtis recalls a night he went boating with Thoreau on
the Concord River to observe the night life of the river. Comments on
the various uses of post offices.

10 [WEISS, JOHN?] Poem Read at the Annual Dinner of the Class of
    Eighteen Hundred and Thirty-Seven. Boston: Deland Printers.
        A poem read by Weiss extolling Thoreau's kinship with nature.
Reprinted in part in TSB, no. 21 (October), p. 5.

                              1875

1   MILLINGTON, Mrs. L.A. "Thoreau and Wilson Flagg." Old and New
    11 (April):460–64.
        A review of The Woods and By-Ways of New England that compares
the writings of Flagg and Thoreau. Thoreau "studied men as he studied
trees, and had a strange pleasure in the discovery of one whose nature
was crabbed and awry," and Flagg "is on neighborly terms with all the
trees." Finds that Flagg copied Thoreau's writing style very closely.

2   HUDSON, HANNAH R. "Concord Books." Harper's Monthly Magazine 51
    (June):28–31.
        Regards Thoreau as half poetical and half mathematical. He
worked with his hand as well as with his head. He went to live at
Walden Pond as a protest against the social order. Discusses the
origin of the name "Walden" and feels that it came from Richard Walden,
an important man in early Massachusetts history.

3   TAYLOR, BAYARD. "A Reminiscence of Thoreau." New-York Daily
    Tribune, 28 August, p. 3.
        Relates the story about the placing of Thoreau's Ktaadn for
publication. The compositor could not make out one word in the

manuscript, took it to the editor, and they decided that the word was "scows" and printed that instead of the intended "aeons." This angered Thoreau, and he wrote a strong letter of protest to Greeley, who had taken the article to Taylor. Reprinted in Cameron, 1973, pp. 284-85.

4 [SANBORN, FRANKLIN BENJAMIN.] "Hudson and Thoreau." Springfield Republican, 28 October, p. 5.
 Writes about the funeral of Frederick Hudson, one-time reporter for the New York Herald, and notes that he used to have a garden near the point where Thoreau kept his boat. The men were most unlike except in their "upright independence and their domestic affections--which in both were warm and noble." Reprinted in Cameron, 1981a, p. 37.

5 BARRON, ALFRED. Foot Notes or Walking as a Fine Art. Wallingford, Conn.: Wallingford Printing Co., 330 pp.
 Barron's writing style is similar to Thoreau's. In the preface he says that whenever he is walking he seems to have an invisible companion. At first he thought that it was the "Evil One" but then thought that it was Thoreau. Part of the preface is reprinted in TSB, 38 (Winter 1952), p. 1.

1876

1 WHIPPLE, EDWIN P[ERCY]. "The First Century of the Republic." Harper's Monthly Magazine 52 (March):525.
 Believes that with all his peculiarities Thoreau was a humorist, scholar, and a poet, "also in his way, a philosopher and a philanthropist." Reprinted: 1876.7.

2 Obituary for Sophia Thoreau. Springfield Republican, 10 October.
 Brief account of Sophia and her family. Original in scrapbook at the Concord Library.

3 [SANBORN, FRANKLIN BENJAMIN.] "Sophia Thoreau." Springfield Republican, 13 October.
 A memorial to both Henry and Sophia Thoreau.

4 BUTTERWORTH, H.W. "Concord Writers." Youth's Companion, 7 December.
 Devotes a section to Thoreau, his life and principles. Believes that his ideas on society and religion were false but appreciates his contributions to natural history and finds his essays full of fine thoughts.

5 ALCOTT, LOUISA MAY. Rose in Bloom. Boston: Roberts Brothers, 375 pp.

1876

    A novel in which one of the characters remarks: "It is the good company I've been keeping. A fellow can't spend a week with Thoreau and not be the better for it."

  6 BURROUGHS, JOHN. <u>Winter Sunshine</u>. New York: Hurd & Houghton, 234 pp.
      Remembers Thoreau's thoughts on walking, autumnal tints and wild apples while adding his own comments.

  7 WHIPPLE, EDWIN P[ERCY]. "The First Century of the Republic." In <u>The First Century of the Republic</u>. New York: Harper & Bros., p. 389.
      Reprint of 1876.1.

1877

  1 H[ARRIS], A[MANDA] B. "Thoreau's Hermitage." <u>New York Weekly Evening Post</u>, 31 January.
      Comments on Thoreau's first essays with a description of Walden Pond, his hut, and his grave.

  2 STEWART, GEORGE, Jr. "Evenings in the Library: No. 2 Emerson." <u>Belford's Monthly Magazine</u> 1 (January):222–34.
      In this article on Emerson the author strongly denounces Thoreau. Emerson, in a letter thanking the author for the article, takes exception to his treatment of Thoreau, saying that he has been under-rated and that he was a superior genius. This letter is printed in Rusk, <u>The Letters of Ralph Waldo Emerson</u>, vol. 6 (New York: Columbia University Press, 1939), pp. 302–3. See 1894.23 for retraction.

  3 M[UNROE], A[LFRED]. "Concord Authors Continued." <u>Richmond County</u> (Stapleton, N.Y.) <u>Gazette</u>, 15 August.
      Considers Thoreau an "indifferent" disciple if not a bold imitator of Emerson. Condemns his poetry as forced and unnatural.

  4 "Letter From Concord." <u>Richmond County</u> (Stapleton, N.Y.) <u>Gazette</u>, 12 September.
      Describes Walden Pond and Thoreau's life there as gleaned from <u>Walden</u>.

  5 FIELDS, JAMES T[HOMAS]. "Our Poet Naturalist." <u>Baldwin's Monthly</u> (September).
      Praises Thoreau's books, saying they can always be read with pleasure and profit. Reviews some of Thoreau's life and notes his closeness with nature: "I used to think I could tell when he was in Boston by a kind of pine-tree and apple-tree odor that preceded him, and accordingly counted on a call that day from him." Recommends that

visitors to Concord look at the house where Thoreau was born on Old
Virginia Road. Notes than on the way one might meet Mr. Emerson, Mr.
Channing, or Mr. Alcott. Remarks on Thoreau's reading habits as shown
by the quotations in his books. Hopes that the day will come when some
publisher will properly print his journals. Reprinted: 1880.23.

6   HUGHES, THOMAS. Review of Page's Thoreau: His Life and Aims.
    Academy 12 (17 November):462–63.
        Appreciates Thoreau's philosophy of simplicity more than the
artificiality of society.

7   COLLINS, MABEL. "Thoreau: Hermit and Thinker." Dublin
    University Magazine 90 (November):610–21.
        Reviews Thoreau's writings, calling them "simple in style and
full of his peculiar earnestness of thought." He does not appeal to
the popular mind, but his ideas will continue to be a power in the
world because of certain readers who feel as he did.

8   Review of Page's Thoreau: His Life and Aims. Athenaeum
    (London), November, pp. 562–64.
        Notes that Thoreau has now been dead for sixteen years. Feels
that Page did his biography in a hasty way. Asks the question: "Did
the individuality of the man naturally lead to the episode that made
him famous, or did the episode engender a false individuality?" Asks
if Thoreau were a true "Child of the Open Air" or play acting in his
Walden story. Considers his admirers not nature lovers but Emersonian
transcendentalists. He symbolizes nature at times and uses "her as a
peg upon which to hang moralizing platitudes about human life." Sums
up feeling that Thoreau was indeed a "Child of Open Air." He
understood, in part, the sophism of the "modern heresy of work." He
understood and loved the wind (the final test of a nature worshiper)
and did not regard animals as dumb; he made friends with them. One is
surprised that after two years he walked away from those friends.

9   "Henry David Thoreau." Christian at Work, 13 December, p.
    961.
        Reviews Page's life of Thoreau and feels that no one has done
more to dispel the misconceptions and prejudices about Thoreau, which
have concealed "the true features of a man of true genius and worth."

10 BURROUGHS, JOHN. Birds and Poets with Other Papers. New York:
    Hurd & Houghton, pp. 37, 48–49, 145–46, 189.
        Feels that Thoreau's Maine Woods is "free from any verbal
tricks or admixture of literary sauce." Recalls that Thoreau said that
the brown thrush's song told the farmer to "drop it" during the corn-
planting season. Notes other Thoreau bird references.

11 LARCOM, LUCY, ed. Hillside and Seaside. Boston: James R.
    Osgood & Co., p. 190.

1877

Reprints Thoreau's "Fisher Boy." The first anthology publication of this poem.

   12 PAGE, H.A. [Alexander Hay Japp]. <u>Thoreau: His Life and Aims</u>.
        Author's edition, from advance proofsheets. Boston: James R.
        Osgood & Co., 234 pp.
          This first English biography of Thoreau treats him kindly and
refutes the adverse criticism that has been leveled against him.
He is one of the early critics to recognize that Thoreau had a sense of
humor. Remarks that a few years before "the name of Thoreau stood to
me for morbid sentiment, weak rebellion, and contempt for society." He
learned with study that this was not true, that the author was a loving
person who had been coated with "stoicism and protest." Asks in this
biography for an unbiased hearing from his readers and tries to write
about him in the same way. A much more thoughtful and coordinated
biography by one who studied and wrote about what he learned, as
contrasted with Channing's (see 1873.12).

   13 ROBINSON, Mrs. WILLIAM S., ed. <u>"Warrington" Pen-Portraits</u>.
        Boston: Mrs. W.S. Robinson, 587 pp.
          Robinson, a classmate and friend of Thoreau, relates
reminiscences including an exact account of the death of John Thoreau.
Prints a review of <u>A Week on the Concord and Merrimack Rivers</u> by
Elbridge Gerry Robinson, pp. 576–77 (see 1849.30).

1878

    1 A[LCOTT], L[OUISA] M[AY]. "In Memorium." Unidentified source
       dated 29 March.
         Verse. Reprinted in Cameron, 1973, p. 306.

    2 ANDERSON, A.D. "Henry David Thoreau." <u>Nassau Literary Magazine</u>
       33 (March):263–71.
         One of the first studies of Thoreau to discover that he was
more than a nature lover. He was also a profound philosopher as well a
philanthropist. Notes that his honesty was as great a feature of his
character as his love of nature and believes that his natural and often
unconscious humor brightens his writings, which are mostly subjective.

    3 [CURTIS, GEORGE WILLIAM.] "A Good Sketch of Thoreau." <u>Harper's</u>
       <u>Monthly Magazine</u> 56 (March):624–25.
         Although Thoreau was little known to the world while he lived,
he is becoming more famous with the years. He was well known in
Concord during his lifetime, but few thought that he was more than a
"queer and incomprehensible character . . . full of odd whimsies." He
was, however, one of the remarkable New England authors. Gives a
firsthand description of his physical appearance. There is no trace of

sentimentality in his books, but his "genius is sweet and clear, and Thoreau was a noble and characteristic product of modern America."

4 [SANBORN, FRANKLIN BENJAMIN.] "Minot Pratt." Springfield Republican, 3 April, p. 4.
    Recalls that both Minot and Thoreau loved nature more than the scientific desire for knowledge; Minot was a "farmer-naturalist" and Thoreau a "poet-naturalist." Reprinted in Cameron, 1977, p. 85.

5 "Concord Celebrities." Springfield Republican, 11 April, p. 8.
    Reports on an Alcott lecture at the home of Joseph Cook. Thoreau could be a good companion when he wanted to be but he was best in a society of one, himself. Notes that there were enough unpublished Thoreau literary remains to fill several volumes. Reprinted in Cameron, 1977, p. 87.

6 "Alcott and His Friends." New-York Weekly Tribune, correspondent's date, 21 April.
    Reports on an Alcott "Conversation" at Rev. Joseph Cook's parlor at the Hotel Bellevue. Thoreau was briefly noted as the first to call John Brown a hero and for giving a talk about him at the town hall after being refused its use by the town selectmen. Reprinted in Cameron, 1973, p. 312.

7 [ILEX, ARBOR.] "Camps and Tramps about Ktaadn." Scribner's Monthly 26 (May):33–47.
    Writes that this author will not follow "Thoreau in his intimate searches in forest life and frontier art and customs." After describing the equipment and provisions for this expedition it is admitted that "Thoreau specifies much more limited fare and wardrobe for this very route."

8 Review of Page's Thoreau: His Life and Aims. Atlantic Monthly 51 (May):672–73.
    Favorably reviews this English biography (1877.12) saying that it was well done, that the biographer had studied carefully all of Thoreau's books. However, the best writing in the book are the quotations from Thoreau, Emerson, and Channing. Finds some of the comparisons extreme, such as Thoreau with St. Francis of Assisi.

9 O'CONNOR, J.V. "Thoreau and the New England Transcendentalism." Catholic World 27 (June):289–300.
    Reviews Page's biography of Thoreau. "Morbid irritability and unwholesome sensitiveness were characteristics of the movement known rather vaguely, as 'New England Transcendentalism.'" Thoreau was the only one who tried out these theories to the fullest extent, "and the incompleteness and failure of his life cannot be concealed by all the verbiage and praise of his biographer."

1878

10 "Old Concord." Journal of Commerce, July.
        Notes that Thoreau is not pronounced Thorreau. The family has
now completely died out with the death of Miss Sophia. Tells the story
about Thoreau's inquiring of an old trapper how to capture a woodchuck
without trapping. The reply was to shoot them. Calls Thoreau's Walden
stay a "fanciful hermitage--that of a hermit who had his cell within a
mile of churches, schools and the haunts of men." In Thoreau's time,
however, it was a lonely lake.

11 BEERS, HENRY A[GUSTIN]. A Century of American Literature: 1776–
        1876. New York: Henry Holt, pp. 294–314.
        Brief biographical sketch followed by extracts from Thoreau's
works.

12 BLISS, PORTER C. "Thoreau." In Johnson's New Universal
        Cyclopedia. Vol. 4. New York: Alvin J. Johnson, p. 842.
        Brief Thoreau biographical sketch. On page 814, vol. 7 of
        1886 revision.

13 LINTON, W.J., ed. Poetry of America. London: Bell, pp. 157–
        59.
        Reprints Thoreau poems "Inspiration" and "Upon the Beach" in
an anthology. Perhaps the first English anthology to include Thoreau
poetry.

14 PEABODY MUSEUM. "III. Thoreau Collection." In Third Annual
        Report, p. 6.
        Paragraph notes that a large collection of Indian implements
"made by the late Henry D. Thoreau" had been deposited at the museum.

15 RICHARDSON, CHARLES F[RANCIS]. A Primer of American Literature.
        Boston: Houghton, Osgood, p. 80.
        Brief section commenting on Thoreau's Walden Pond life and on
his books.

16 SANBORN, FRANKLIN BENJAMIN. Memoirs of John Brown. Concord,
        Mass.: Printed by J. Munsell, Albany, N.Y., pp. 45, 50.
        Remembers that he introduced John Brown to Thoreau, Emerson,
and others and they were impressed. In March 1857 Brown dined with
Thoreau, who was then living with his family near the railroad station.
"The two idealists, both of them in revolt against the civil
government, because of its base subservience to slavery, found
themselves friends from the beginning." Emerson joined the two later.

1879

1 [McCREARY, E.D.] "A Worshiper of Nature." National Repository
        5 (June):525–34.

Reviews Thoreau's life and parentage. In college he rebelled against some of the routine curriculum, devoting much of his time to the study of pre-Shakespearian English poets. His pursuit of a solitary life began during his school years, but his interest in nature did not come until later. Notes that he was much more attuned to nature than a normal person, proving this by numerous quotations from his writings. Considers that his retreat to Walden was not for solitude but to learn what was superfluous in modern civilization.

2   STONE, Z.E. "General Jackson in Lowell." Contributions to the
    Old Resident's Historical Association of Lowell 1 (June).
        Recalls listening to Thoreau lecture on his way of life,
which some Concordians thought was just "lying around mother earth,
indolently watching the active squirrels." Reprinted in part in TSB,
no. 78 (Winter 1962), p. 4.

3   COLLYER, ROBERT. "Henry Thoreau." Unity, 1 August.
        Relates the visit that Thoreau made to him in June 1861 on
his way to Minnesota. Describes Thoreau as "rather slender, but of a
fine mold, and with a presence which touched you with a feeling of
perfect purity, as newly opened roses do. And it was a clear rose-
tinted face he turned to you, delicate to look at as the face of a
girl, and the great grey eyes, full of quiet sunshine." Comments on
the reasons he feels Thoreau went to Walden. Reprinted: 1879.6.

4   "Thoreau's Thoughts / An Evening in Concord among the Pearls of
    Henry Thoreau." Boston Daily Advertiser, 7 August.
        Reports on the reading of some of Thoreau's unpublished
journals by H.G.O. Blake at Alcott's summer School of Philosophy.
Alcott also gave his impressions of Thoreau. Reprinted in Cameron,
1977, pp. 96–98.

5   "The Philosophers at Concord." Springfield Republican, 11
    August, p. 4.
        Reviews the Concord School of Philosophy program, noting that
Walton Ricketson, who as a boy knew Thoreau, brought to the school a
life-size medallion head of the author. This sculpture will remain at
Orchard House until the school closes. Reprinted in Cameron, 1981a,
p. 6.

6   COLLYER, ROBERT "Henry Thoreau." Christian Register, 16 August,
    p. 1.
        Reprint of 1879.3.

7   "Hawthorne Upon Thoreau." Harper's Weekly 23 (1 November):863.
        Prints a letter from Hawthorne to Epes Sargent, editor of the
New York Mirror, urging him to publish Thoreau's writings: "the man
has the stuff to make a reputation of, and I wish that you might find
it consistent with your interest to aid him in obtaining that object."

1879

8   GREYLOCK, GODFREY [J.E.A. Smith]. Taghconic; the Romance and
    Beauty of the Hills. Boston: Lee & Shepard, pp. 248–49, 254–
    56.
        Tells of Thoreau's climbing Greylock. Quotes a long passage
about the break of day from the summit.

9   HIGGINSON, THOMAS WENTWORTH. "Thoreau." In Short Studies of
    American Authors. Boston: Lee & Shepard, pp. 22–31.
        Strongly defends Thoreau against Lowell's criticism, writing
that he finds it difficult to be patient with Lowell and what seems to
be his "wanton misrepresentations." Lowell applies the word indolent,
"but you might as well speak of the indolence of a self-registering
thermometer. . . . The impression that Thoreau was but a minor Emerson
will in time pass away, like the earlier classification of Emerson as a
second-hand Carlyle."

10 Historical Sketch of the Salem Lyceum, with a List of the
    Officers and Lecturers since Its Formation in 1830. Salem:
    Press of the Salem Gazzette.
        Lists under "Twentieth Course. 1848–49" two Thoreau lectures:
"Student Life in New England, Its Economy" and "Student Life, Its Aims
and Employments." Reprinted in ATQ, no. 14 Supplement 2 (Spring 1972),
pp. 5–25.

11 JAMES, HENRY, Jr. Hawthorne. English Men of Letters Series.
    London: Macmillan, pp. 93–95.
        James continues Lowell's denunciation of Thoreau with:
"whatever question there may be of his talent, there can be none of his
genius. It was a slim and narrow one, but it was eminently personal.
He was imperfect, unfinished, inartistic; he was worse than provincial-
-he was parochial; it is only at his best that he is readable."

12 McGuffey's Fifth Eclectic Reader. Cincinnati: Van Antwerp,
    Bragg & Co.
        Brief biographical sketch noting that Thoreau has few if any
superiors in descriptive ability. Gives extracts from "The Succession
of Forest Trees" under the title "Transportation and Planting of
Seeds."

13 RUSSELL, A.P. Literary Notes. New and rev. ed. Boston:
    Houghton, Osgood, pp. 93–95, 136–37.
        Quotes Thoreau on doing good and the relationship of clothing
to one's life work.

14 Semi-Centennial. Proceedings of the Fiftieth Anniversary of the
    Organization of the Concord Lyceum, Tuesday, January 7, 1879.
    Concord: Tolman & White.

Notes that in 1840 Thoreau as secretary wrote that "a small
audience having assembled, owing to the inclemency of the weather, the
lecture from Mr. Keyes was deferred till the next meeting, and in
accordance with a vote of the Lyceum, Mr. William S. Robinson read the
Message of Governor Morton." Gives the list of lecturers at the
Lyceum, including Thoreau who gave 19 lectures. Reprinted in ATQ, no.
14 supplement 2, (Spring 1972), pp. 26–34.

1880

1 WILTON, MURIEL. "Thoreau." Golden Rule, 14 April.
    Verse. Reprinted in Cameron, 1958, p. 16.

2 HOSMER, JOSEPH. "Henry D. Thoreau." Concord Freeman: Thoreau
    Annex, 6 May, pp. [1–2].
        Relates that he had recently moved from Concord to
Chicago and was frequently asked if he knew Thoreau. Often the
inquirer thought that Thoreau took to the woods because he was "jilted"
by the girl he loved. Notes that he was little known even by his own
townspeople. His collected works are in the public library of Chicago,
and, as some of the volumes are nearly worn out, they apparently are
well read. Extracts from several of his books follow. Reprinted in
Cameron, 1958, pp. 7–15.

3 "The Thoreau Engravings." Concord Freeman: Thoreau Annex, 6
    May, p. [3].
        Comments on the quality of the engravings used in the Annex.
Reprinted in Cameron, 1958, p. 15.

4 "James Very." Boston Sunday Herald, 16 May, p. 10.
        Notes that Very had much in common with two American authors,
Thoreau and Dana, because all three were Americans who were not too
strongly influenced by foreign literature.

5 JAPP, ALEXANDER H[AY]. "Thoreau's Pity and Humor." Spectator 53
    (12 June):749–50.
        In a letter to the editor, Japp points out the reasons
Stevenson did not accurately assess Thoreau's character and ability
(see 1880.6).

6 STEVENSON, ROBERT LOUIS. "Henry David Thoreau." Cornhill
    Magazine 41 (June):665–82.
        The opening sentence of this article is an indication of its
tenor: "Thoreau's thin, penetrating, big-nosed face, even in a bad
woodcut, conveys some hint of the limitations of his mind and
character." This article was reprinted many times in influential
periodicals in 1880 and did much to retard proper recognition of
Thoreau. Reprinted in Glick, 1969, pp. 65–88.

1880

7   L[ATHROP], G[EORGE] P[ARSONS].   "Thoreau and Shakespeare."   New
York Evening Post, dateline 22 July.
        Reports that after a lecture on Shakespeare by Denton J.
Snyder of St. Louis there was discussion about Thoreau's reasons for
his Walden retreat, noting that Shakespeare retired in middle life to
Stratford for the peace of the country.   Reprinted in Cameron, 1974,
pp. 44–45.

8   ALBEE, JOHN.   "At Thoreau's Cairn, Walden Woods, 1879."   Journal
of Speculative Philosophy 14 (July):338.
        Verse on Thoreau's Walden stay.

9   [CONWAY, MONCURE.]   "Thoreau's Pity / From a Letter to the
Speculator."   Unidentified newspaper, July.
        Refutes Stevenson's comment in 1880.6 that "there is no trace
of pity in Thoreau" by describing an incident involving a runaway
slave.   Reprinted in Cameron, 1958, p. 146.

10   "Concord Conversations."   Springfield Republican, 4 August.
        Notes that in the Hawthorne talk Thoreau felt that man
had no miseries except those he created himself: indigestion and
laziness.   Both Thoreau and Hawthorne had a vein of humor, but Thoreau
has "no more love for fiction in books than in character."   Reprinted
in Cameron, 1958, p. 62.

11   [SANBORN, FRANKLIN BENJAMIN.]   "A Cause of Thoreau Revival."
Springfield Republican, 4 August, p. 4.
        The literary men in Paris, London, and New York are again
beginning to notice Thoreau's writings.   Comments on the many recent
discussions of the author at the Concord School of Philosophy.
Reprinted in Cameron, 1981a, pp. 45–46.

12   "Concord Philosophers."   Boston Evening Traveller, 12 August.
        Reports that H.G.O. Blake read unpublished selections from
Thoreau's journals.   Reprinted in Cameron, 1974, p. 73.

13   GUERRIER, GEORGE P.   "Thoreau and the Summer School of Philosophy
/ Editor of the Traveller."   Boston Evening Traveller, 13 August.
        The writer replies to a question put to him the night before
at the School of Philosophy: "Would it be possible to follow out,
seriously, a scheme of life such as exhibited in Walden?"   His answer:
"Let the novice beware not to take in too literal a manner 'Life at
Walden.'"   Reprinted in Cameron, 1974, p. 25.

14   "Thoreau: The Poet-Naturalist."   Springfield Republican,
14 August.
        Reviews Blake's readings from Thoreau's unpublished
journals at the Concord School of Philosophy on 11 August.   Reprinted
in Cameron, 1977, pp. 107–10.

15 [BLAKE, HARRISON GRAY OTIS.] "Thoreau and Solitude." Home
    Journal, 15 August.
        Uses numerous Thoreau quotations to prove that he was not a
misanthrope. Is happy that he turned aside from the usual paths and
committed himself "not to institutions, but to the end which these have
in view, to simple living, to thought, to intercourse with nature and
the highest human society whether in books or people."

16 "New Bits from Thoreau's Journal." New-York Daily Tribune, 15
    August, p. 7.
        Blake read a series of extracts from Thoreau's unpublished
journals at the Concord School of Philosophy that he had copied for his
own use before he knew that he was to be willed the Thoreau papers.
Reprinted in Cameron, 1974, pp. 87-89.

17 "Mr. Alcott on Thoreau." Concord Freeman, 19 August, p. [8].
        Defends Thoreau in a lecture at the School of Philosophy on
12 August against the remarks of a lecturer, Mr. Denton J. Snider, who
said that he was a disordered genius. Calls him an extreme individual-
ist who was named after Thor, who said: "I will find a way or cut
one." Considers that "he had high ideals and rare poetic gifts. He
was more in sympathy with nature than any other human being." Notes
that Blake read more unpublished extracts from Thoreau's journals.

18 FLAGG, WILSON. "Symposium of Mystics." Boston Evening
    Transcript, August.
        Regards Emerson's writing style as not new but that of the
Elizabethan era. Of all of the Emerson imitators Thoreau was the most
successful and "has certainly outdone him in absurdity." Examples of
the two writers' words follow to prove the point of similarity.
Reprinted in Cameron, 1974, pp. 49-50.

19 [MEAD, EDWIN D.?] "Philosophy at Concord II." Nation 31 (2
    September):164-66.
        Reviews Blake's readings from Thoreau's unpublished
manuscripts at the Concord School of Philosophy. Concludes that
Thoreau's attitude toward society "was neither iconoclastic or
whimsical, but simply expressed private incommensurability with the
average taste in ethics and character." Reprinted in Cameron, 1974, p.
76.

20 KENNEDY, WILLIAM SLOANE. "A New Estimate of Thoreau." Penn
    Monthly 11 (October):794-808.
        Strongly rebukes Lowell, Henry James, Jr., and others for not
looking objectively at Thoreau's works. In his own appraisal he writes
that "the influence of his rugged energy, his fine idealism, the purity
and honesty, and manliness of his life, shall for generations breathe
through the literature and the life of America like a strengthening

1880

ocean breeze, adding tone, toughness, elasticity, and richest Attic
sparkle to the thought of men." Reprinted in Glick, 1969, pp. 90-106.

  21 MILLARD, BAILEY. "Influence of Thoreau and His Writings on
        Robert Louis Stevenson." San Francisco Examiner, date unknown.
           In certain ways, Stevenson's philosophy was similar to
Thoreau's. Their attitudes toward conventionality and nature were
nearly alike. "Their view of life and the way man should regard life
accord in all essentials. They pursued the same lines of study with
widely dissimilar methods but both arrived at the same conclusions."

  22 BARTLETT, GEORGE B. The Concord Guide Book. Boston: D.
        Lothrop, pp. 60, 63-65.
        Describes the various Thoreau residences in Concord.

  23 FIELDS, JAMES T[HOMAS]. "Our Poet-Naturalist." In Papyrus
        Leaves. Edited by William Fearing Gill. New York: R.
        Worthington, pp. 31-36.
        Reprint of 1877.5.

  24 SCUDDER, HORACE E[LISHA], ed. "Henry D. Thoreau." In American
        Prose. Boston: Houghton, Osgood, pp. 296-365.
           In an introduction Scudder briefly reviews Thoreau's life
and books. States that the chief value of Walden lies not in its
philosophy but in its observation of the facts of the world around us.
Dislikes Thoreau's almost insolent manner of presenting his thoughts.
Says that "there is a rudeness which seems sometimes affected, and a
carelessness which is contemptuous," yet "he reaches a force and energy
which are refreshing." Reprints of "Sounds" and "Brute Neighbors" from
Walden and "Highland Light" from Cape Cod follow.

1881

  1 BURROUGHS, JOHN. "Thoreau's Wildness." Critic 1 (26 March):74-
      75.
        Calls Thoreau the wildest New Englander since the Indians left
that area. He relates the author's life and habits to that of the red
man, "an Emersonian or transcendental red man." Reprinted in Harding,
1954, pp. 87-90.

  2 SANBORN, F[RANKLIN] B[ENJAMIN]. "Thoreau's Unpublished Poetry."
      Critic 1 (26 March):75-76.
        After Thoreau's sister, Sophia, died in 1876 Sanborn was
willed Thoreau's four volumes of Dial. In one of these he found a
sheet of Thoreau's unpublished verse. Some of these poems are printed
in this article together with a reproduction of an ambrotype of Thoreau
made at New Bedford. Reprinted: 1882.35.

3   "Thoreau's Portrait--By Himself." Literary World 12 (26 March):
     116-17.
         Reviews Early Spring in Massachusetts and finds it commendable
because it is Thoreau's self-drawn portrait and can not be misunder-
stood.

4   K[ENNEDY], W[ILLIAM] S[LOANE]. "Portraits of Thoreau with a
     Beard." Critic 1 (9 April):95.
         States that the ambrotype noted in 1881.2 is not the only
bearded portrait of Thoreau and mentions two others taken earlier.

5   DALL, CAROLINE HEALY. Buffalo Daily Courier, 14 April.
         The publication of Early Spring in Massachusetts brings to
Dall memories of twenty-five years before, when she met Thoreau after
delivering a lecture in Concord. She was asked by Thoreau to spend a
day with him, which she did much to her enjoyment. Reprinted in part
in TSB, no. 62 (Winter 1958), p. 1.

6   "Thoreau's Journal." New York Independent, 14 April.
         Reviews Early Spring in Massacusetts. Thoreau was not well
known when he was alive and will not be now that he is dead, but many
of his work ought to be kept alive because there is merit in them.

7   SANBORN, F[RANKLIN] B[ENJAMIN]. "Henry David Thoreau." Harvard
     Register 3 (April):214-17.
         Summarizes the highlights of Thoreau's life and reproduces a
full-page portrait of him.

8   "Review of Early Spring." Yale Literary Magazine 46 (May):353-
     54.
         Finds this volume lacks much of the vivacity of life and
"charming freedom" of Thoreau's other books. Agrees that this is to
be expected in journals that are but a "collection of neat little
thumb-sketches."

9   FLAGG, WILSON. "Sayings / Written in the Style of Emerson,
     Alcott and Thoreau." Boston Evening Transcript, 12 July.
         Flagg writes aphorisms in the styles of these authors.
Reprinted in Cameron, 1974, p. 103.

10 "The Concord School / Dr. Jones's Lecture and Readings from
     Thoreau's Manuscripts." Boston Daily Advertiser, dateline 19
     July.
         After the lecture Blake gave some of his impressions of
Thoreau and read more unpublished selections from the journal.
Reprinted in Cameron, 1974, p. 119.

1881

11   "Concord Philosophy. Mr. Blake's Reading from Thoreau." Boston
     Traveller, 20 July.
        Reports on Blake's talk on Thoreau and readings from the
unpublished journal. Reprinted in Cameron, 1974, p. 121.

12   "Reading from Thoreau." Boston Evening Transcript, 20 July.
        Reports Blake's impressions of Thoreau's character and
readings from the manuscripts. Reprinted in Cameron, 1974, p. 119.

13   "Thoreau's Relation to His Time." Boston Daily Advertiser, 4
     August.
        Reviews at length a talk on Thoreau at the Concord School of
Philosophy, in which the speaker, H.G.O. Blake, tells how he personally
related to some of Thoreau's philosophy. Reprinted in Cameron, 1974,
p. 145.

14   KING, ISABELLA "Early Spring." Harvard Register 3:233–34.
        Reviews the book saying "it is elevating as well as enter-
taining to notice the difference in tone that characterizes the
differences in time."

15   BLAKE, H[ARRISON] G[RAY] O[TIS], ed. Introduction to Early
     Spring in Massachusetts. Boston: Houghton, Mifflin, pp. iii-
     vii.
        Describes how he composed the book by combining Thoreau's
notes for the same day of the month for succeeding years to point out
the changing life in nature. Comments on Thoreau's philosophy.

16   COOKE, GEORGE WILLIS. Ralph Waldo Emerson: His Life, Writings,
     and Philosophy. Boston: James R. Osgood, pp. 83–85, 106, 112,
     159, 232.
        Various comments about Thoreau and Emerson.

17   FIELDS, ANNIE. James T. Fields: Biographical Notes and Personal
     Sketches. Boston: Houghton, Mifflin, pp. 101–2.
        Quotes from Fields's diary on a visit to Mrs. and Miss Thoreau
after Thoreau's death to discuss the publication of his journals. Miss
Thoreau was not in any hurry to have them published.

18   FLAGG, WILSON. "Thoreau." In Halcyon Days. Boston: Estes &
     Lauriat, pp. 164–68.
        Reprint of 1872.7.

19   PORTER, NOAH. Books and Reading or What Books Shall I Read and
     How Shall I Read Them? New York: Charles Scribner's Sons, pp.
     70, 119.
        Feels that Thoreau's philosophy varies from the Christian
gospel and that his writings along with those of other "advanced

thinkers" show lack of faith in the importance of the Christian
history.

1882

1 REID, Rev. STUART J. "A Summer Day at Concord, Massachusetts."
   Manchester Quarterly (England), no. 1 (January), pp. 1–13.
       Reid, an Englishman, writes that Julian Hawthorne encouraged
him to visit Concord when he came to America. Notes that he found the
village was correctly named because of its peaceful aspect. Visited
Walden Woods, where "Thoreau was dreaming the best years of his
romantic life away in undimmed communion with the trees and flowers and
birds, which he loved so well." Stopped at the School of Philosophy
and found on one of its walls a portrait of Thoreau.

2 "Emerson's Home." Utica (N.Y.) Daily Press, 2 May, p. 4.
       Describes Emerson's home, where Thoreau "was daily visitor";
"his 'Wood Notes' might have been unuttered but for the kind encourge-
ment he found there."

3 "Thoreau and Greeley." New-York Daily Tribune, 11 June, p. 5.
       Prints many letters from Greeley to "Friend Thoreau."
Introduces the letters with comments about the beginning of Greeley-
Thoreau friendship in 1843. The letters deal with the various Thoreau
manuscripts that Greeley was attempting to place, and with the payment
when placed. The letters are annotated. Notes that in March 1856
Greeley asked Thoreau to be the tutor of his children, but after much
thought the offer was rejected.

4 [SEDGWICK, A.G.] "Thoreau." Nation 25 (13 July):34–35.
       Reviews Sanborn's Henry D. Thoreau, which may be "considered a
vindication, a criticism, a eulogy, or a biography; and in no one of
those aspects is it a very successful literary performance."

5 "Concord and Thoreau." Literary World 13 (15 July):227–28.
       Reviews Sanborn's biography of Thoreau disapprovingly, saying
"the author, whether he laid out his work so from the first, or whether
a great part of the outer half was put in front after the inner was
well framed and already under his hand, and put in because this seemed
too scant, has made fairly good work of it all."

6 J[ANVIER], T.A. "Review of Sanborn's Life of Thoreau." American
   4 (15 July):218.
       Believes that Sanborn was faced with two serious difficulties
in writings this biography: first, Thoreau's life was completely devoid
of those interesting adventures and incidents that are necessary for a
good biography; and second, his biography had already been written.

1882

7   "Thoreau." <u>Boston Evening Transcript</u>, 19 July.
     More than many law-abiding and sober citizens, Thoreau
accomplished what he set out to do by developing all of his best
faculties to the highest degree.

8   "Henry D. Thoreau." <u>Christian Union</u>, 20 July.
     Reviews Sanborn's <u>Life of Thoreau</u>. Concludes it has no real
merit because it is the result of a sympathetic treatment that does not
give a true picture.

9   "Emerson and Thoreau." <u>Boston Herald</u>, 23 July.
     Notes that Mr. Albee gave an account at the School of
Philosopy of his meeting in 1852 with Emerson and Thoreau. Reprinted
in Cameron, 1974, p. 202.

10 "Reminiscences of Emerson." <u>New-York Daily Tribune</u>, 23 July, p.
    4.
     Reviews a paper read by John Albee at the Concord School of
Philosophy containing his college notes on a visit to Emerson and
Thoreau. Says that Emerson was fond of Thoreau, but is not sure
whether in a human way or in an amusing way. Reprinted in Cameron,
1974, p. 204.

11 "Philosophy at Concord." <u>Boston Traveller</u>, 24 July.
     John Albee spoke on his first meeting with Emerson and
Thoreau. Reprinted in Cameron, 1974, pp. 208-9.

12 "The School of Philosophy." <u>Boston Journal</u>, 24 July.
     Reports that Sanborn introduced Albee, who read a paper on an
interview that he had with Emerson and Thoreau in 1852. Reprinted in
Cameron, 1974, p. 209.

13 "Mr. Sanborn's <u>Thoreau</u>." <u>Critic</u> 4 (29 July):197-98.
     Deals harshly with the biography; feels that it exaggerates
the importance of Thoreau and that it is padded with petty, irrelevant
material that tends to take away from an objective picture of
the man.

14 BURROUGHS, JOHN. "Henry D. Thoreau." <u>Century</u> 24 (July):368-79.
     Notes that Thoreau's fame is beginning to increase as it was
certain to do. His reputation is still in the bud, and "its full leaf
and flowering are not yet, perhaps not in many years to come." Admits
that Thoreau was not a scientific naturalist because he did not have
the detective eye needed. Tries to refute both Stevenson's accusation
that Thoreau was a skulker and Emerson's regret that he had not
engineered for all America instead of being the captain of a
huckleberry party.

15 "The Concord Philosophers / Selections from Thoreau's Unpublished
    Manuscripts." Boston Journal, 3 August.
        Sanborn read more of Thoreau's writings, interspersing them
with personal comments. Read some of Thoreau letters written in 1843
while he was with Emerson's brother on Staten Island. Reprinted in
Cameron, 1974, p. 236.

16 "Concord Philosophy / Readings from Thoreau's Original
    Manuscripts." Boston Daily Advertiser, 3 August.
        Reports that Sanborn read a work in three chapters that did
not follow a single thought but was filled with aphorisms and witty
sayings that brought Emerson to the minds of many. This was followed
by the reading of several personal Thoreau letters, written when he was
staying at Staten Island, giving his impressions of New York City.
Reprinted in Cameron, 1974, pp. 235–36.

17 "Philosophy at Concord / Interesting Readings from Unpublished
    MSS. of Thoreau." Boston Traveller, 3 August.
        Reports on Sanborn's readings from Thoreau's "The Service,"
which was rejected by Margaret Fuller for the Dial. Reprinted in
Cameron, 1974, pp. 234–35.

18 "Childhood: An Evening with Thoreau." Boston Evening Transcript,
    4 August.
        Sanborn reads from Thoreau's unpublished manuscripts.
Reprinted in Cameron, 1974, p. 237–38.

19 "Philosophy at Concord / Emerson and Thoreau Readings."
    Springfield Republican, 6 August, p. 6.
        At the Concord School of Philosophy Sanborn read "the most
Platonic and Transcendental things from the youthful manuscripts of
Henry Thoreau." Reprinted in Cameron, 1981b, p. 15

20 [SANBORN, FRANKLIN BENJAMIN.] "The Correspondence of Emerson and
    Thoreau." Springfield Republican, 7 August, p. 2–3.
        Reports that Thoreau's letter to his sister, Helen, dated 27
October 1837, and his poem "Fall of the leaf" were read at the School
of Philosophy. Reprinted in Cameron, 1981a, p. 50.

21 "The Concord School." Inter Ocean, 9 August.
        Reviews Sanborn's lecture on Thoreau at the Concord School of
Philosophy in which he read from unpublished manuscripts, noting that
the "popular belief that Thoreau devoted his life to hunting, fishing,
walking, etc. is only a partial and limited view of the man."
Reprinted in Cameron, 1974, p. 239.

22 POWERS, H.N. "Thoreau." Dial 3 (9 August):70–71.
        Reviews Sanborn's Henry D. Thoreau with the conclusion that
Thoreau will never be widely read. If his life is viewed merely as a

1882

protest against worldliness and insincerity; it will have a good
influence even though it is unpractical in many regards.

23 [SANBORN, FRANKLIN BENJAMIN.] "An Anthology of American Prose /
    Includes Whittier, Emerson and Thoreau Characteristics."
    Springfield Republican, 14 September, pp. 2–3.
        Reviews the book that was published some years ago under the
title American Prose. Notes that it publishes passages from Walden
and Cape Cod but overlooks his most poetical book, A Week on the
Concord and Merrimack Rivers. Uses the bearded portrait of Thoreau
made in 1861. Reprinted in Cameron, 1981a, p. 51.

24 [CURTIS, GEORGE WILLIAM.] "Editor's Easy Chair." Harper's
    Monthly Magazine 65 (September):631–32.
        Reviews Sanborn's Thoreau. Calls it a vivid picture of
Concord's unique character as well as a contribution "to the village
history of New England, which is the key to our national development."

25 [WHIPPLE, EDWIN PERCY.] "Some Recollections of Ralph Waldo
    Emerson." Harper's Monthly Magazine 65 (September):581–82.
        Relates how Emerson introduced him to Thoreau and the story
about Thoreau and Alcott outside a Concord saloon. Finds Sanborn's
Thoreau interesting because Sanborn knew him so intimately that he
gives an inside picture of the man.

26 PURVES, JAMES. "Review of Sanborn's Life of Thoreau." Academy
    22 (14 October):271–72.
        Reviews the book favorably and notes that Thoreau "appeals to
many of us who want to live their own lives in their own way."

27 WATTS-DUNTON, THEODORE. Review of Early Spring in Massachusetts
    and Sanborn's Life of Thoreau. Athenaeum, 28 October, pp. 558–
    60.
        Considers Thoreau too self-conscious to really know nature,
which never gives up her secrets to one "who can never look at her with
the frank eyes of a child, but looks at her with the eyes of a bookish,
self-improving, transcendental species. . . . In prose, however,
Thoreau has said most wise and beautiful things, and he will always
retain a place in literature."

28 EVERETT, A. N. Boston Evening Transcript, unknown date.
        Believes that students will always appreciate Thoreau and
discuss him. Like literary persons will "extend to him the hand of
friendship and enroll his name to the others dear to fame."

29 "Sanborn's Thoreau." Boston Daily Advertiser, undated clipping.
        Reviews Sanborn's book. Considers that it approaches Thoreau
with a lack of perspective that occurs in small towns "where a Channing

seems a Milton or a Dante, and Thoreau a Virgil." Feels that Thoreau does not deserve such a tribute, for he was a small man in reality. Reprinted in Cameron, 1974, p. 186.

30 ALCOTT, AMOS BRONSON. Ralph Waldo Emerson: An Estimate of His Character and Genius: In Prose and Verse. Boston: A. Williams, pp. 55, 59-67.
   Remarks about Thoreau. Prints a poem, "Ion: A Monody," in which Thoreau and Emerson are identified as Ion and Hylus.

31 ALCOTT, AMOS BRONSON. Sonnets and Canzonets. Boston: Roberts Brothers, pp. 119, 121.
   Prints two poems about Thoreau: "Who Nearer Nature's Life Would Truly Come" and "Much do They Wrong Our Henry, wise and Kind."

32 CONWAY, MONCURE DANIEL. Emerson at Home and Abroad. Boston: James R. Osgood, pp. 279-89.
   Writes that Thoreau was "twice born" because during his college years he began to change from conformity to independent thought.

33 Memorial of George Washington Hosmer, D.D. Edited by the children of Hosmer. Privately printed, p. 23.
   Notes that the Hosmer lands have entertained noble guests including Thoreau, "who haunted them at morn and eve, piercing with his quickened sense to the fine occult essence in grass-blade, in dew-drop, and pine cone and icicle."

34 NICHOL, JOHN. "Henry David Thoreau." In American Literature: An Historical Sketch. Edinburgh: Adams & Charles Black, pp. 313-21.
   Quotes Emerson and Lowell opinions. States that Thoreau has been favored with many reviews, some competent, some incompetent, but "little else than water added to the wine of Emerson and Lowell." Lowell is "active to restlessness, practical, and almost fiercely patriotic" while Thoreau is "lethargic, self-complacently defiant and too nearly a stoic-epicurian adiaphorist to discompose himself, in party or even in national strifes." Considers his Excursions interesting and unique but feels that he condemns civilization.

35 SANBORN, F[RANKLIN] B[ENJAMIN]. Essays from "The Critic." Boston: James R. Osgood.
   Reprint of 1881.2.

36 SANBORN, F[RANKLIN] B[ENJAMIN]. Henry D. Thoreau. American Men of Letters Series. Boston: Houghton, Mifflin, 324 pp.
   As reviews have indicated, this biography has merits but many defects. Sanborn gives firsthand impressions of Thoreau as he knew

1882

him. He includes much irrelevant material that has little or no
relationship to Thoreau's life. He includes many previously
unpublished Thoreau letters and college essays, all of which bear the
heavy hand of Sanborn's editing. Present-day Thoreau scholars agree
that there is a wealth of information in the biography but that it must
be carefully doublechecked for accuracy.

37 STEWART, GEORGE, Jr. "Thoreau: The Hermit of Walden." In
  Transactions of the Literary and Historical Society of Quebec.
  No. 16. Quebec: Printed at the Morning Star, pp. 121–51.
     Prints a paper read by Stewart before the Society on 2 March
1882, commenting on Thoreau's heritage and life at Walden, with
quotations from his writings.

38 WELSH, ALFRED H. Development of English Literature and Language.
  Chicago: S.C. Griggs, pp. 409–14.
     Analyzes Thoreau's English and concludes that it comes from
the poets and prosewriters in their best days. "His metaphors and
images have the freshness of the soil," and yet "one cannot fail to see
the resemblance of his style to Emerson's and Alcott's."

1883

1 F., E.M. [Mrs. Jean Munroe Le Brun]. "Henry Thoreau's Mother."
  Boston Daily Advertiser, 14 February.
     In a letter to the editor, Mrs. Brun takes Sanborn to task for
writing in his biography that Thoreau's mother was a gossip. Admits
that she was a great talker, but she was not uncharitable and few women
did more good and less harm than she did. Reprinted in Cameron, 1977,
p. 113.

2 "Thoreau's Example." Spectator (England) 56 (17 February):239–
  40.
     Reviews the English edition of Sanborn's Life of Thoreau.
Regards the book as "too slight to merit much praise" but considers
Thoreau's Walden years as "Liberty expressed in the clearest language."

3 BURROUGHS, JOHN. "Signs and Seasons." Century 25 (March):672–
  82.
     Compares Thoreau and Gilbert White, noting that the landscape
of each became a part of them; that was the charm of Walden and of
White's writings. "These men stayed at home; they made their nests,
and took time to brood and hatch." Says that Thoreau was for years
trying to find the first expression of spring after a long New England
winter.

4 "The Philosophical Trinity / Readings from Thoreau." Springfield
  Republican, 30 July, pp. 4–5.

Mr. Blake prefaced his reading from Thoreau's manuscripts with the remark that thus far this year the Concord School lectures had been "so abstract, metaphysical, and carefully thought out, it seemed a sort of incongruity to read anything from Thoreau here and particularly from his journal; his way of thinking and study being so different." Reprinted in Cameron, 1981b, p. 23.

5 NICHOLS, F.A. "Readings from Thoreau's Manuscripts." Boston Evening Transcript, 3 August, p. 6.
      Reviews the Concord School readings from Thoreau followed by a conversation on the meaning of some of the sentences. Reprinted in Cameron, 1981b, pp. 37–42.

6 "The Concord School." Boston Herald, 12 August, p. 4.
      Does not consider the school as actually a school of philosophy because it largely depended on the writings of Hawthorne, Emerson, and Thoreau finding "these more attractive than the severer pursuits of philosophy." Believes this was its weakness and the reason for its decline. Reprinted in Cameron, 1981b p. 61.

7 "Extracts from Thoreau's Journal." Literary World 14 (8 September):287.
      Reports on the Concord School readings without comment.

8 "The Famous Concord." Utica (N.Y.) Daily Press, 8 September, p. 3.
      Describes Thoreau's house at Walden Pond and his grave at Sleepy Hollow Cemetery.

9 WOODRUFF, Class of '85. "Henry D. Thoreau." Nassau Literary Magazine 39 (October):161–64.
      Thoreau is not a scientist, philosopher, or poet but "presents a strange, unaccountable mixture of the three."

10 ALBEE, JOHN. "Thoreau." In Poems. New York: G.P. Putnam's Sons, p. 83.
      Verse.

11 ALBEE, JOHN. "Reminiscence and Eulogy" and "Readings from Thoreau's Manuscripts." In Concord Lectures on Philosophy. Edited by Raymond L. Bridgman. Cambridge, Mass.: Moses King, pp. 67–68, 124–26.
      Comments that Emerson considered that there was no real American literature. Said we need great writers and poets and was always looking for them. In a conversation "Thoreau said he had found one, in the woods, but it had feathers and had not been to Harvard." Reprinted from 1882.10. Also reports on Sanborn readings from Thoreau's unpublished manuscripts, including "The Service," which was rejected by Margaret Fuller for publication in the Dial.

1883

12 CARLYLE, THOMAS. The Correspondence of Thomas Carlyle and Ralph
    Waldo Emerson. Edited by Charles Eliot Norton. 2 vols. Boston:
    James R. Osgood, 2:130–31, 185.
         Thoreau is mentioned in two Carlyle letters to Emerson dated
    18 May 1847 and 13 August 1849. Carlyle was not enthusiastic about
    Thoreau's work.

                              1884

1 "Thoreau's Summer." Critic, 21 June.
        Considers the chief interest of Thoreau's writings to be his
   pertinent or impertinent observations, which show him as clearly as his
   notebooks reveal the habits of the animals and birds he studied. The
   writings are slightly depressing in tone. "He seems to be 'whistling
   to keep his courage up.' . . . He was a sad man and a lonely one."

2 UNDERWOOD, SARA A. "Thoreau's Summer." Index 4 (26 June):615.
        Likes the book and says that "every new work bearing the
   impress of Thoreau's name more and more impresses the reader with the
   sense that his writings are destined to live."

3 "Thoreau in Summer." Literary World 15 (12 July):223.
        Notes that "a striking portrait of Thoreau is to be seen
   between the lines." Appreciates the complete index.

4 B[LACKWELL], H[ENRY] B. Review of Summer. Women's Journal, 26
   July, p. 244.
        Recommends the book for "quiet reading in the open air during
   summer vacation."

5 "Poetry at the Concord School. Thoreau's Poetical Favorites."
   Springfield Republican, 30 July.
        Because Channing did not appear as scheduled, Sanborn read
   some of Channing's poetry and some passages from his biography of
   Thoreau. Notes that Emerson first became attracted to Thoreau by his
   poem "Sic Vita." Reprinted in Cameron, 1974, p. 282.

6 SHATTUCK, HARRIETTE R. "Thoreau and Channing." Boston Evening
   Transcript, 30 July.
        Sanborn read from Channing's life of Thoreau, followed by a
   discussion of Thoreau by those who knew him. Elizabeth Palmer Peabody
   noted that "in the most trifling things his life was as beautiful as
   the clear-cut marble. Like the ornaments on the Gothic cathedral he
   was perfect in the most trifling details." Reprinted in Cameron, 1974,
   p. 284.

7 "Yesterday's Exercises / Emerson and Thoreau." Unidentified
   newspaper, 30 July.

Sanborn read from Channing's life of Thoreau. In the following discussion Miss Peabody told of occurrences while Thoreau lived with the Emersons. Reprinted in Cameron, 1974, p. 283.

8 Review of Summer. Nation 39 (31 July):98–99.
Considers that Thoreau is greatly overrated and this book is an example of the "narrow range of his misanthropic spirit." Feels that the main point of his life was a repetition from year to year, without growth, merely with a change of season.

9 HAWTHORNE, JULIAN. "Scenes of Hawthorne's Romances: Concord." Century Magazine, n.s. 5 (July):380–97.
Remarks that strangers are coming to visit the site of Thoreau's hut twenty years after his death. Some of these pilgrims are obnoxious and have queer ideas about Thoreau and his life. Many thought that Sleepy Hollow Cemetery was by Walden Pond, that Emerson lived at Thoreau's hut, and that Thoreau was present at the Battle of Concord.

10 HOLLAND, F.M. "Emerson and the Concord School of Philosophy." Index 16 (7 August): 63–64.
Notes that while Thoreau did not care about money, he did his best to make a good bargain when it was for someone else.

11 BARNARD, WILLIAM F. "A Day in Old Concord." Marlboro (Mass.) Advertiser, 27 August.
Includes comments on Thoreau in his discussion of Concord.

*12 SMITH, ERWIN F. "Thoreau's Note Books." Grand Rapids (Mich.) School Moderator, 4 September.
Reviews Early Spring in Massachusetts and Summer. Listed in TSB, no. 22 (January 1948), p. [4].

13 LEWIN, WALTER. Review of Summer. Academy (London) 26 (27 September):193–94.
Compares Thoreau with Gilbert White and concludes that there is an important difference. White loved to study plants and animals, while Thoreau studied them because of his love for them. Thoreau's interest was centered in man, not nature. As a student of life, he went to the woods because living there seemed simpler and truer than town life.

14 JORDAN, DAVID STARR. Indiana Student 11:53.
Notes that Thoreau might have directed large enterprises but preferred his huckleberry parties. Agrees with Thoreau's philosophy for it is easier to find captains of industry than pioneers in science.

Writings about Henry David Thoreau, 1835–1899

1884

15 BLAKE, H[ARRISON] G[RAY] O[TIS]. Introduction to Summer from the Journal of Henry D. Thoreau. Boston: Houghton, Mifflin, pp. iii–v.
    Remarks on the unfavorable criticism of Thoreau as a naturalist and his love of nature. Notes that Thoreau might have been contemplating such a book when he wrote in his journal that "a book of the seasons, each page of which should be written in its own season and out of doors, or in its own locality, wherever it may be."

16 EMERSON, RALPH WALDO. "Thoreau." In Lectures and Biographical Sketches. Boston: Houghton, Mifflin, pp. 419–52.
    A short poem followed by Emerson's funeral address as printed in the Atlantic Monthly for May 1862.

17 HAGUE, WILLIAM. Ralph Waldo Emerson. New York: Putnam, p. 12.
    Tells a story about Thoreau's remark about a dentist.
Reprinted in TSB, no. 38 (Winter 1952), p. 3.

18 HAWTHORNE, JULIAN. Nathaniel Hawthorne and His Wife. 2 vols. Boston: James R. Osgood, 2:468–69 and passim.
    Julian notes that his mother wrote in a letter of 3 October 1852 that Thoreau's hut was still standing near the edge of the pond, on a level spot surrounded by pine trees.

19 HIGGINSON, THOMAS WENTWORTH. Margaret Fuller Ossoli. Boston: Houghton. Mifflin, p. 134 and passim.
    Disagrees with Henry James, Jr., who called Thoreau parochial. States that "when Thoreau studies birds and bees, Iliads and Veta, in his little cottage by Lake Walden, to look out of the little world into the great, that is enlargement; all else is parochialism."

1885

1 JAPP, A[LEXANDER] H[AY]. "Thoreau." Spectator (London) 58 (24 January):122–23.
    Believes that nothing that Thoreau wrote will be remembered for long, but his fight for individual freedom will live on.

2 BARTON, W[ILLIAM] G. "Thoreau, Flagg, and Burroughs." Essex Institute Historical Collections 22 (January–March):53–80.
    A short biography of Thoreau followed by comparisons with Flagg and Burroughs. "Thoreau rouses; Flagg soothes; Burroughs stimulates and gratifies."

3 "Thoreau, Unpublished Notes Read to the Concord School." Boston Daily Advertiser, 25 July.

Reports on a lecture on Thoreau by Blake, in which he read from the journals.

4   "Thoreau's Wild Wood Philosophy." <u>New-York Daily Tribune</u>, 26 July, p. 2.
     Reports that Blake read from Thoreau's unpublished manuscripts at the Concord School of Philosophy. Long quotations are printed.

5   COOKE, GEORGE WILLIS. "<u>The Dial</u>: An Historical and Biographical Introduction with a List of the Contributors." <u>Journal of Speculative Philosophy</u> 19 (July):225–65, 322–23.
     Cooke prepared a full account of the <u>Dial</u> that was to preface a reprint of the sixteen issues by Roberts Brothers. This project was abandoned but was revised as a book and published in 1902.

6   Report of the Concord 250th Anniversary. <u>Boston Evening Transcript</u>, 19 September.
     Reviews a speech given by James Russell Lowell saying that "we are indebted to Mr. Thoreau . . . for another lesson, almost as important; and that is, that nature is as friendly, as inspiring, here as in Wordsworth's country, or anywhere else."

7   BARTLETT, GEORGE B. "Concord Men and Memories." <u>Bay State Monthly</u> 3 (September):224–32.
     Presents a short history of Concord and Thoreau's part in it.

8   BARTLETT, GEORGE B. "Thoreau." In <u>Concord, Historic, Literary, and Picturesque</u>. Boston: D. Lothrop, pp. 72–75.
     Guidebook sketch of Thoreau's life and homes.

9   BURROUGHS, JOHN. <u>Fresh Fields</u>. Boston: Houghton, Mifflin.
     Notes that although Thoreau was graduated from Harvard he never lost his love for the wild because he was a "wood-genius--the spirit of some Indian poet or prophet." Reprinted in the Wake-Robin edition (New York: Wm. H. Wise, 1924), p. 44.

10 DERBY, J.C. <u>Fifty Years among Authors, Books and Publishers</u>. Hartford, Conn.: M.A. Winter, p. 624.
     Lists Thoreau with Ticknor and Fields authors but in the index lists him as "H.J. Thoreau."

11 ELIOT, GEORGE [pseud.]. <u>George Eliot's Life</u>. 2 vols. Edinburgh and London: William Blackwood & Sons, 1:41
     Mentions Thoreau in a letter dated 29 June 1856 to Miss Sara Hennell.

12 HOLMES, OLIVER WENDELL. <u>Ralph Waldo Emerson</u>. American Men of Letters Series. Boston: Houghton, Mifflin, pp. 72, 86 and passim.

79

1885

Dislikes Thoreau's philosophy and way of life. Calls him "the nullifier of civilization, who insists on nibbling his asparagus at the wrong end."

13 SANBORN, FRANKLIN BENJAMIN. The Life and Letters of John Brown. Boston: Roberts Brothers, 645 pp.
    Mentions Thoreau's connection with the Brown verdict.

14 SANBORN, KATE. The Vanity and Insanity of Genius. New York: George J. Combes, pp. 89–91.
    Repeats Thoreau's mother's remark when told that her son's style was like Emerson's: "Yes, Mr. Emerson does write like my son."

15 STEDMAN, EDMUND CLARENCE. Poets of America. Boston: Houghton, Mifflin, p. 336.
    Comments on Lowell's treatment of Thoreau, saying "his analysis of Thoreau is sharply criticized as being too narrow, but it did expose the defective side of a unique character, and all things considered is the subtlest of his minor reviews."

1886

1 BENTON, JOEL. "The Poetry of Thoreau." Lippincott's Monthly Magazine 37 (May):491–500.
    Does not feel that Thoreau's poetry "will lift the reader by any lyric sweep, but it appeals rather to the inner spirit, like the lines of Wordsworth and Emerson."

2 "Summer School / At Lake Walden." Boston Daily Advertiser, 24 July.
    Reports that several students went by boat to Thoreau's Cove, Walden Pond, where they were told interesting stories about Thoreau by George Bartlett. Reprinted in Cameron, 1974, p. 320.

3 SALT, HENRY S. "Henry D. Thoreau." Temple Bar 78 (November): 369–98.
    Considers Thoreau a prophet trying to warn the world of its path to destruction and, like Whitman, the "incarnation of all that is free, healthy, natural." Walden "deserves to be a sacred book in the library of every cultured and thoughtful man." Reprinted: 1887.8.

4 TALBOT, CHARLES REMINGTON. "Romulus and Remus." Wide Awake 24 (December 1886):49–55; (January 1887):105–11; (February):171–79; (March):234–42; (April):297–305; (May):362–71.
    Serialized story of two young men, disciples of Thoreau, who spend time at a Massachusetts pond.

5 DIRCKS, WILL H. "Thoreau." Introductory note in English edition of <u>Walden</u>. London: Walter Scott, pp. vii–xxviii.
　　Describes Thoreau's heritage, the house in which he was born, his parents, and sketches of his life. Notes that as a diarist he can be compared to Henri Amiel with some thirty volumes of journals. In his life "he adopted poverty like a piece of business" but would not be pecuniarily endebted to anyone. Describes his physical appearance as his friends saw him.

6 HASKINS, DAVID GREENE. <u>Ralph Waldo Emerson: His Maternal Ancestors</u>. Boston: Cupples, Upham, pp. 119–22.
　　Haskins, a Harvard classmate of Thoreau, writes that in college Thoreau gave no indication of any literary or scientific interest. He did not write for any college publication nor belong to any of its scientific societies. In a short time after college days he was completely transformed. He had come under Emerson's influence and became a prototype of him in manner of speaking, expressions, and even the pauses and hesitations in his talking. Haskins says that when he was with both men and closed his eyes he could not tell which one was talking.

7 LONGFELLOW, SAMUEL. <u>Life of Henry Wadsworth Longfellow</u>. 2 vols. Boston: Houghton, Mifflin, 1:142–43.
　　Quotes from Longfellow's journal for 29 June 1848 that he read Thoreau's account of his one night in the Concord jail.

8 MERRIAM, CLINTON HART. <u>The Mammals of the Adirondack Region</u>. New York: Henry Holt, p. 139.
　　Writes that the moose was a favorite hunting game in the Adirondacks until it was exterminated in about 1861. Notes that "in the fall of 1853 Thoreau met an Indian named Tahmunt Swasen, in the forest near Moosehead Lake, Maine, who told him that he had hunted moose in the Adirondacks in New York, but they were more plentiful in the Maine woods." A footnote states that this information came from <u>The Maine Woods</u>, p. 141.

9 MORRIS, CHARLES. "Ascending Ktaadn." In <u>Half-Hours with the Best American Authors</u>. Vol. 2. Philadelphia: J.B. Lippincott, 2:39.
　　Notes in a short biography preceding a sketch from <u>The Maine Woods</u> that Thoreau avoided humans not because he disliked their companionship but rather because the secrets of nature attracted him more.

1887

1 [SANBORN, FRANKLIN BENJAMIN.] "Henry Did Read Ruskin." <u>Springfield Republican</u>, 18 January, p. 2.

1887

Refutes the idea that Thoreau never read Ruskin by showing
that <u>Modern Painters</u> delighted him "partly for the style--for he was an
appreciator as well as a master of style--and partly for the positive,
paradoxical and whimsical nature of the writer."

2　SALT, HENRY S.　"Henry D. Thoreau."　<u>Eclectic Magazine</u> 45
　　(January):89-98.
　　　Thoreau was not advocating isolation from all of the
improvements of society.　He agreed that the civilized state was to be
desired over the savage condition.　He tried, however, to show that
too many artificial wants have not been a blessing but rather a curse
to the human race.　He shows a practical and easy way to overcome this
difficulty: simplify.

3　"Great Day at Concord."　<u>Boston Evening Post</u>, 26 July.
　　　Thoreau is quoted during a discussion, at the School of
Philosophy picnic, on Aristotle's thoughts on friendship.　Reprinted in
Cameron, 1974, p. 353.

4　"The Philosopher's Picnic."　Unidentified newspaper, 27 July.
　　　At the picnic Sanborn read a paper entitled "Thoreau and
Alcott."　Reprinted in Cameron, 1974, p. 353.

5　SHATTUCK, HARRIETTE.　"Field Day for Philosophers."　Unidentified
　　newspaper clipping, 27 July.
　　　Reports that Sanborn spoke on Thoreau and Alcott.　Reprinted
in Cameron, 1974, p. 355.

6　[SANBORN, FRANKLIN BENJAMIN.]　"Thoreau is Our Country's Persius
　　and Ovid."　<u>Springfield Republican</u>, 30 August, p. 2.
　　　In previewing Thoreau's <u>Winter</u> Sanborn notes that this volume
will be modeled after <u>Spring</u>, <u>Summer</u>, and <u>Autumn</u>.　Although he includes
<u>Autumn</u> in the list of the previously published volumes, it was not
published until 1892.　Reprinted in Cameron, 1981a, p. 62.

*7　"In the Woods; One Chapter from the Book <u>Walden or Life in the
　　Woods</u>.　<u>Novoe vremja</u> [New Time], 15 October.
　　　Perhaps the first of Thoreau's writings to be translated into
Russian.　Source:　<u>TSB</u>, no. 150 (Winter 1980), p. 1.

8　SALT, HENRY S.　"Henry D. Thoreau."　<u>Critic</u>, 26 November, 3
　　December, pp. 276-78, 289-91.
　　　Reprinted from 1886.3.

9　JAPP, ALEXANDER H[AY].　"Henry David Thoreau."　<u>Welcome</u> (London)
　　14 (November):652-56.
　　　Finds in Thoreau's <u>Walden</u> shared sympathies written in fine
prose, its occasional acidity giving "additional flavour or relish,

like the sweet-sourness of some wild fruits." This discovery of
Thoreau led to a closer examination resulting in correspondence with
Sanborn, Fields, Walton Ricketson, and other Americans. Ricketson in
one of his letters tells of the New Bedford ambrotype of Thoreau taken
at his father's request. All this gathered information was first
recorded in Thoreau: His Life and Aims (Boston: James R. Osgood,
1877).

10 "Winter Studies / New Selections from Thoreau." New-York Daily
    Tribune, 26 December, p. 6.
        Reviews Winter, saying that no one knew nature's habits better
than Thoreau.

11 BARROWS, CHARLES M. "Henry David Thoreau." In Acts and
    Anecdotes of Authors. Boston: New England Publishing, pp. 463-
    64.
        Biographical sketch of Thoreau noting that he was well
educated, an Oriental scholar with none of the social qualities that
draw men together, and that he kept aloof from his fellow beings.

12 BEERS, HENRY A. "Henry David Thoreau." In An Outline Sketch of
    American Literature. New York: Chautauqua Press, pp. 143-48.
        Biographical sketch followed by an analysis of Thoreau's
philosopy. Decides that "the most distinctive note . . . is his
inhumanity." Tries to find meaning in Ktaadn and the waves of Cape
Cod. Transcententalism was apprehended on the mystical side. He was a
close examiner of nature and has many followers.

13 CABOT, JAMES ELLIOT. A Memoir of Ralph Waldo Emerson. 2 vols.
    Boston and New York: Houghton, Mifflin, 2:282-84.
        Comments on the Emerson-Thoreau relationship and notes that
"Thoreau had a grave, measured way of speaking, and a carriage of the
head that reminded one of Emerson and seemed like unconscious imitation
and in his writing there is often something that suggests this."

14 CARPENTER, EDWARD. England's Ideal. London: Swan Sonnenschein,
    pp. 13-14, 16.
        Relates Walden to the Fabian ideal of reducing life to its
simplest terms. Thoreau protested the artificiality of life in
literature as one of the main dangers of this complex society.

15 CONWAY, MONCURE D[ANIEL]. Pine and Palm. New York: Henry Holt,
    p. 53.
        Describes in a novel how Thoreau rescues an escaped slave from
a Boston mob.

16 GILCHRIST, HERBERT. Anne Gilchrist: Her Life and Writings.
    London: T. F[isher] Unwin, p. 237.

1887

Records that Whitman liked Thoreau but felt that he was
morbid. Thought he went to Walden not because he loved the woods but
because he disliked humanity.

17 HAGUE, WILLIAM. *Life Notes or Fifty Year's Outlook*. Boston:
    Lee & Shepard, p. 187.
    Hague tells of an incident while leaving a dentist office and
meeting Emerson. Hauge told him he was getting his mouth repaired, and
Emerson then related what Thoreau said when he had the same experience.

18 HARRIS, ARMANDA B. "Henry David Thoreau; and Other 'Out-of-Door'
    Writers." In *American Authors for Young Folks*. Boston: D.
    Lothrop, p. 163–82.
    Review's Thoreau's ancestry, his life, and his works,
interspersed with quotations from his writings. Notes that he started
a trend of nature writing in America, naming Wilson Flagg, Colonel
Higginson, Theodore Winthrop, John Burroughs, and several others who
followed Thoreau's lead.

19 MILBURN, W.H. *The Royal Gallery of Poetry and Art*. New York:
    N.D. Thompson, p. 541.
    Identifies Thoreau as a poet and naturalist with solitary
habits and an independent mind whose writings "betray the profound seer
and thinker."

20 PORTER, Rev. EDWARD G. *Rambles in Old Boston, N.E.* Boston:
    Cupples, Upham, p. 117.
    Gives information on the Boston home of John Thoreau, Sr.

21 *Portraits and Biographical Sketches of Twenty American Authors*.
    Number B of Riverside Literature Series. Boston: Houghton,
    Mifflin, no pagination.
    Woodcut portrait of Thoreau with a two-page biography.

22 RICHARDSON, CHARLES F. *American Literature, 1607–1885*. 2 vols.
    New York & London: G.P. Putnam's Sons, 1:385–95.
    Brief biographical sketch. Notes that he has been called
Emerson's leading pupil but retained his independence. He examined
nature more closely than anyone else. Reviews his nine volumes.
Considers *Walden* and *Cape Cod* as most outstanding of his works. Finds
Sanborn's life of Thoreau "a record in which, in thoroughness,
painstaking accuracy, and hearty enthusiasm leaves nothing lacking on
the biographer's part—is a photograph of Thoreau, taken in 1861."
Discusses his poety and prose writing with quotations.

23 WHIPPLE, EDWIN PERCY. *American Literature and Other Papers*.
    Boston: Ticknor, pp. 111–12.
    Concludes that Thoreau was, in his peculiar way, a philanth-
ropist and a philosopher as well as a humorist, poet, and scholar.

24 WHIPPLE, EDWIN PERCY. Recollections of Eminent Men. Boston:
    Ticknor, pp. 134–35.
        Believes that nature was as much a part of Thoreau's life as
religion is to that of others. His every word displays manliness,
sincerity, and courage.

25 WILLIAMS, HENRY, ed. Memorials of the Class of 1837 of Harvard
    University. Boston: Geo. H. Ellis, pp. 37–43.
        Biographical sketch of Thoreau and his ancestry, with notes
about his college years. Remarks on the popular feeling that Thoreau
aped Emerson in all his actions and words, but concludes that this was
not true; any resemblance was just on the surface.

26 WILSON, JAMES GRANT, and JOHN FISKE, eds. Appleton's Cyclopedia
    of American Biography. 6 vols. Philadelphia: D. Appleton,
    6:100–101.
        Biographical sketch of Thoreau's life and works.

                              1888

1 "Thoreau's Winter Journal." Literary World 19 (7 January):4.
        Reviews Winter with the comment that "seen from the outside
it is indeed forbidding, a veritable chestnut burr sure to prick the
fingers of the unwary, but there is enticing meat within if only one
knows how to get at it."

2 [SANBORN, FRANKLIN BENJAMIN.] "Thoreau, Emerson, and Thomas
    Browne." Springfield Republican, 31 January, pp. 2–3.
        Believes that Thoreau was inspired by Sir Thomas Browne and
provides quotations to prove it. Reprinted in Cameron, 1981a, p. 63.

3 KELLY, M.J. "A Visit to Thoreau's Haunts." Genius 1
    (January):21–23.
        Tells of a visit of two boys who made a trip to Walden Pond in
1866 and were dismayed at the merry-go-rounds, dancing platforms, and
lunch tables. Asked a man at the picnic grounds for the location of
Thoreau's hut. He had never heard of it. They discovered the site by
looking at the cut of the hut in their copy of Walden. Reprinted as
Thoreau Society Booklet, no. 14, (1959).

4 "Winter." Nation 5 (January):19.
        Review stating that enough has been written about Thoreau's
philosophy and his application of it. One can see in this book how he
held to these principles and what it failed to do for him as well as
what it did.

1888

5 "Thoreau's Winter Journal." Critic, 3 March.
        Reviews the new book, finding that Thoreau often writes
about music.

6 ALLEN, GRANT. "Sunday at Concord." Fortnightly Review 49
        (May):675-90.
        Allen spent a few days at Concord. Writes that he cannot
feel quite sure that Thoreau was completely sincere, noting that those
who knew him say that he was, while he, knowing him only through his
books, finds a suspicion of insincerity in the turn of some of his
sentences.

7 New York Commercial Advertiser, 12 July.
        Notes that there is a general interest in Thoreau as a nature
writer, but he is not considered a philosopher. Claims that Thoreau's
ideas are of "no use to anybody nowadays," but his nature studies have
"enduring and great value."

8 P., A.H.   "In Winter with Thoreau." Unitarian Review 30
        (July):73-83.
        Reviews Winter, commenting that Thoreau was "a poet, a
moralist, and an affectionate student of nature. He was also a master
of words, whose condensed and clear-cut sentences appeal alike to
lovers of beauty, lovers of strength and inquirers into the reasons of
things."

9 UNDERWOOD, FRANCIS H.   "Henry David Thoreau." Good Words 29
        (July):445-52.
        Thoreau has to be one author in ten thousand for whom so much
has to be overlooked or tolerated, and yet he is read with delight.

10 KENNEDY, WILLIAM SLOANE. "Concord Recollections: Some Fresh
        Remembrances of Emerson, Alcott and Thoreau." Boston Evening
        Transcript, 15 September, pp. 8-9.
        Discovers that he did not understand Thoreau's character until
he saw his picture. This revealed to him the secrecy of his life
through the poetlike delicacy of his features. "He was too sensitive
and ideal in his nature to endure patiently the roughness and brutality
of the world."

11 ZABRISKIE, F.N. "Brown Bread and Baked Beans." Lippincott's
        Magazine 42 (October):518-31.
        Humorously discusses Boston and its environs, including
Concord and its writers. Notes Walden Pond, "where Henry D. Thoreau
built his hut and played hermit for two years, making himself think
that he was fiercely independent of human kind, whereas we all know now
that he was unconsciously posturing with an unerring instinct and
appetite for 'appreciation.'"

12 BAKER, ISADORE. "On receiving a Violet from the Grave of
    Thoreau." In A Collection of Poems by America's Younger Poets.
    Philadelphia: Westminster.
        Sonnet.

13 BESANT, WALTER. The Eulogy of Richard Jefferies. London:
    Chatto & Windus, pp. 221–25.
        Compares Thoreau with Jefferies, noting that neither had
any scientific training, both lived simply, and neither went to church
but was religious in his own way. Their faces were similar but in
height Thoreau was short and Jefferies tall.

14 BLAKE, H[ARRISON] G[RAY] O[TIS], ed. Introduction to Winter.
    Boston: Houghton, Mifflin, pp. iii–vi.
        Feels that Thoreau took little part in politics, trade, the
church, and society's institutions generally because he felt that
they were a hindrance to his true life. He was constantly thinking
about an ideal friendship.

15 EMERSON, EDWARD WALDO. Emerson in Concord. Boston: Houghton,
    Mifflin, 266 pp.
        Describes the first meeting of Emerson and Thoreau and
discounts the impression first created by Lowell that Thoreau imitated
Emerson. Admits that living under the same roof, Thoreau may have
picked up some tricks of voice or expression from Emerson, but if so,
it was unconsciously acquired. Describes the building of a rustic
summer house for Emerson by Alcott and Thoreau.

16 GARNETT, RICHARD. Life of Ralph Waldo Emerson. London: Walter
    Scott, pp. 157–59.
        Writes that Thoreau was an ally of Emerson, who took a half
paternal, half-fraternal interest in him. Without Emerson "Thoreau
might never have existed as the Poet-Hermit of Walden."

17 LAMPLOUGH, EDWARD. "Thoreau's Walden." In Hull and Yorkshire
    Frescoes: A Poetical Year Book of 'Specimen Days.' Printed for
    private circulation. Hull: Charles Henry Barnwell, p. 362.
        Contains a poem for each day of the year, with each dedicated
to a subscriber. "Thoreau's Walden" was under 12 December and for Rev.
W.B. FitzGerald, the Manse, Prestwich, Manchester. Reprinted in TSB,
no. 66 (Winter 1959), p. 2.

18 SALT, HENRY S. Literary Sketches. London: Swan Sonnenschein,
    pp. 124–66.
        Reprint of 1886.3.

19 SHARP, WILLIAM. "Henry D. Thoreau." In Encyclopedia Britannica.
    9th ed. Vol. 23. Edinburgh: Adams & Charles Black, pp. 313–14.

1888

Comments that Thoreau was "one of the most strongly-marked individualities of modern times. . . . His weakness as a philosopher was his tendency to base the laws of the universe on the experience-born, thought-produced convictions of one man--himself. His weakness as a writer is the too frequent striving after antithesis and paradox. If he had all of his originality without the itch of appearing original, he would have made his fascination irresistible."

20 SIDNEY, MARGARET. <u>Old Concord: Her Highways and Byways</u>. Boston: D. Lothrop, pp. 77–85.
     Describes Thoreau's Walden Pond hut, his life and philosophy.

21 TALBOT, CHARLES F. <u>Romulus and Remus: A Dog Story</u>. Boston: D. Lothrop, 217 pp.
     Thoreau is a character in this children's story.

1889

*1 PERKINS, FREDERICK. "Nature in Thoreau and Burroughs." <u>Collegian</u>, February, pp. 119–26.
     Listed in <u>TBS</u>, bibliography, no. 104 (Summer 1986), p. 4.

 2 BURROUGHS, JOHN. "Henry David Thoreau." <u>Chautauquan</u> 9 (June):530–33.
     An appreciation of Thoreau, with a brief biography. Considers Thoreau and John Brown as kindred spirits: "two shafts shot from the same bow, but at different targets."

 3 "A Week on the Concord." <u>Saturday Review</u> 68 (17 August):195–96.
     Review of the English edition of <u>A Week on the Concord and Merrimack Rivers</u> commenting that here Thoreau presents his peculiar philosophy with much more geniality and much less straining after exaggerated effect than in his other books.

 4 FLUGEL, EWALD. "Ein Brief Emerson's." <u>Anglia</u> 12 (1889): 454–59.
     Prints an Emerson letter to Charles Stearns Wheeler that notes that Thoreau has been invited to tutor the children of his brother, William, at Staten Island. Thoreau "cine der anzichendsten gestalten ger amerikenischen literureschichte. Aufsatze iiber Emerson (Works X, 421–452; Lectures etc.) und von Lowell, Study Windows (ed. Garnett 1887, pp. 137–152)"; followed by works of other authors who have written about Thoreau. Reprinted in Cameron, 1973, pp. 28–29.

 5 ABBOTT, CHARLES C[ONRAD]. <u>Days Out of Doors</u>. New York: D. Appleton, pp. 98, 169.
     Notes Thoreau's comment about the white oaks in Concord retaining their leaves and quotes his verse on the vireo.

6 BURROUGHS, JOHN. "Henry D. Thoreau." In Indoor Studies.
   Boston: Houghton, Mifflin, pp. 1–42.
       Thoreau was a crusty person who delighted to walk in all kinds
of weather. He liked the "flavor of strong racy men" such as Whitman.
He was fond of using hyperbole and exaggeration to make his point.
Considers the journals as published by Blake experimental. "There is
an attempt to make something out of nothing by mere force of words."
Concedes, however, that they contain interesting and valuable notes on
nature. Defends Thoreau against the name "skulker," saying that if he
had stayed with pencil-making the world would have lost some of "the
raciest and most antiseptic books in the English literature." "Thoreau
was, probably, the wildest civilized man this country has produced."

7 CHENEY, EDNAH D[OW], ed. Louisa May Alcott: Her Life, Letters,
   and Journals. Boston: Roberts Brothers, p. 98.
       Louisa May Alcott reports in her diary that on Monday Emerson,
Thoreau, Sanborn, and Pratt carried the body of Louisa's sister, Beth,
out of her home to Sleepy Hollow Cemetery. Beth died 14 March 1858.

8 DIRCKS, WILL H. Prefatory note to the English edition of A Week
   on the Concord and Merrimack Rivers. London: Walter Scott, pp.
   v–xviii.
       Discusses the transcendentalist movement and Thoreau's relat-
ionship to it. Notes that in this book his observations on nature are
not those of a naturalist or scientist but rather of a literary person.
Contrary to the statements of Lowell, Thoreau did have his own brand of
humor.

9 FROTHINGHAM, OCTAVIUS BROOKS. In Appletons' Cyclopedia of
   American Biography. Vol. 6. New York: D. Appleton, pp. 100–101.
       Short biographical sketch of Thoreau, with portrait. Comments
that his religion was transcendental in that the element of negation
was great. In a pagan fashion he wrote hymns to the night.

10 HUBERT, PHILIP G., Jr. In Liberty and A Living. New York: G.P.
   Putnam's Sons, pp. 163–90.
       This writer is convinced that the time will come when Thoreau
will be listed with the greatest American authors. "He was the first
noted Protestant—passionate, earnest, persistent, honest—against the
sordid materialism of this country."

11 SANBORN, JOHN WENTWORTH. "Observations of Henry Thoreau." In Go
   To the Ant. Cincinnati: Cranston & Stowe, pp. 76–80.
       Reprints "The Battle of the Ants" from Thoreau's Walden, with
an explanatory preface.

12 SMYTH, ALBERT H. "Henry David Thoreau." In American Literature.
   Philadelphia: Eldredge & Brother, pp. 85–87.

1889

        Brief biographical sketch with comments on his books and
style. Notes that his writing is like that of Emerson in points of
style and in the short sentence packed with meaning.

   13 STEDMAN, ARTHUR. "Henry David Thoreau." In A Library of
       American Literature. 11 vols. New York: Charles L. Webster,
       1889-91, 6:323-38.
          Notes the birth and death dates of Thoreau. Publishes excerpt
from Walden, two poems, and "The Wellfleet Oysterman."

                              1890

   *1 "Henry David Thoreau." London Evening Post, 10 January.
          Listed in Allen, p. 129.

    2 JONES, S[AMUEL] A[RTHUR]. "Thoreau: A Glimpse." Unitarian 5
       (January):18-20; (February):65-68; (March):124-25.
          Applauds Thoreau's ideals in a paper delivered before the
Unity Club of Ann Arbor, Michigan, on 2 December 1889. Strongly
defends him against such adverse critics as Lowell. Reprinted:
1890.23.

    3 WOODBURY, CHARLES J. "Emerson's Talks with a College Boy."
       Century Magazine 29 (February):626-27.
          Finds that there was something "catching" about Emerson if one
came under his spell. Thoreau did, and his manner of speaking was so
nearly like Emerson's that it was difficult to separate the two in conversation. Thoreau was made by Emerson, as if he were own his child.
Remarks that Emerson talked often and tenderly of Thoreau. Gives
quotes from their conversations, including some well-known stories.
Reprinted: 1890.28.

    4 RANDOM, RODERICK. "Letters to Men of Note. To Walt Whitman, in
       America." Wit and Wisdom, 17 May, pp. 20-21.
          Whitman's poetry came upon England "as something new, strange
and unmeasured. . . . There was nothing in Democracy so painted that
we should desire it. It has no softness, no comeliness, no fine
upholstery, no cushion. . . . It was a return to barbarism. Such
things might do for simpletons like Thoreau and Walt Whitman but as for
us who had knowledge of Mayfair, and had tasted the good things
thereof, we begged to be excused." Simplicity is fine for those who
like it, but others do not care for it.

    5 BROWN, DARLING JOSEPH. "Henry B. [sic] Thoreau." Piscataquis
       (Me.) Observer, 22 May, pp. 20-21.
          Describes the placing of a new monument on Thoreau's family
plot at Sleepy Hollow Cemetery by his relative, B.B. Thatcher of
Bangor, Maine. States that it was fitting that the monument was made

of granite from Maine because that was one of Thoreau's favorite states. Reprinted in TSB, no. 37 (October 1951), p. 3.

6 SALT, HENRY S. "Thoreau's Poetry." Art Review (London) 1
   (May):153-55.
       Writes that only a few of his poems have been printed, and
   those scattered in his books and in the Dial. Hopes that a fuller
   collection will be published. His models in style were some minor
   Elizabethan poets--Donne, Herbert, Quarles, and others of the same
   style. Prints some of his poems and feels they may be the keys to
   unexplained parts of his writings. "Sympathy" was about the love that
   he gave up for his brother, "Inspiration" was the awakening of
   his transcendentalism. Considers that there was good as well as bad
   poetry published in the Dial. After his thirtieth year he gave up
   poetry writing because of Emerson's faint praise. He was a poet in the
   larger sense.

7 SALT, HENRY S. "Thoreau's Anti-Slavery and Reform Papers."
   Lippincott's Magazine (English ed.), (August):277-83.
       Reviews some of the major events that shaped Thoreau's
   character. Notes that whenever principle was at stake his "will was as
   inflexible as the cast iron to which Hawthorne compared him."

*8 L., A. "In Thoreau's Country." New York Evening Post (Weekly),
    10 October.
        Listed in Allen, p. 129.

9 "The Life of Thoreau." London Standard, 16 October, p. 2.
       Notes there are now three biographies of Thoreau as well
   as numerous articles about him, but does not feel that the bibliography
   is yet complete. He was "a man whom it was impossible not to like even
   to love," but he did little for the world. Other naturalists,
   White, Jefferies, and others "found the world and its responsibilities
   quite compatible with the study of bird and beast and flowers."
   Thoreau looked at everything as a transcendentalist. He cared nothing
   for others' opinions. His works, with the exceptions of Walden,
   Excursions, and Letters, have no immortality. His poems do not have
   music. Most of his other writings could have been written by a "much
   feebler philosopher." Considers Thoreau's biography is in his books.
   Salt's biography is unnecessary except for those who do not want to
   read his books. Had he seen more of the world he would have been less
   interesting and not as original. "He did admirable service in teaching
   his countrymen that there are higher ideals in life than dollars and
   trotting horses."

10 TOLMAN, GEORGE. "Letter to the Editor." Boston Evening
    Traveller, 17 October.

1890

The letter states that the new Thoreau monument in Sleepy
Hollow Cemetery was made possible by a bequest from Aunt Maria Thoreau
to Mr. Thatcher of Bangor.

11 JAPP, A[LEXANDER] H[AY]. "Thoreau's Life." Spectator (London)
    65 (18 October):526-28.
       Reviews Salt's biography of Thoreau. Comments on the
shortcomings of the other biographies of him.

12 LEWIN, WALTER. Review of Salt's Life of Thoreau, and of Anti-
    Slavery and Reform Papers, edited by H.S. Salt. Academy
    (London) 38 (25 October):357-58.
       Comments that thirty years ago Thoreau's philosophy was
little regarded. Today it is discussed in the drawing room as well as
in the study. His writings should be considered, for he was a poet, a
naturalist, and an independent thinker.

13 "Thoreau." Speaker 2 (8 November):529-30.
       Reviews Salt's Life of Thoreau and his Anti-Slavery and Reform
Papers.

14 DIRCKS, WILL H. "The Life of Thoreau." Newcastle Daily Leader
    (England), 25 November.
       Reviews Salt's biography of Thoreau.

15 YEATS, WILLIAM BUTLER. "The Lake Isle of Inisfree." National
    Observer, 13 December.
       In this poem Yeats shows the influence of Thoreau by wishing
to go to the shore of Inisfree, build a small cabin, grow beans and
have a hive of bees. Here he will find peace. Reprinted: 1892.27.

16 OTTER, J.L. "Thoreau." Nature Notes: The Selborne Society
    Magazine, 1 (15 December):185-88.
       Considers Thoreau's view of nature optimistic in that it
is working to a gracious and wise end. "Joy is the condition of life."

17 "New Books and New Editions / The Life of Henry David Thoreau."
    Animal World (London) 21 (December):186-87.
       The first page of this publication shows "the Forest of
Walden, where, retreating from the busy world, Thoreau built a hut and
made a home, his only companions being the wild animals, trees, and
plants around him." Gives lengthy quotations from the biography.
Considers Walden a transcendental retreat for Thoreau as Brook Farm was
to others. Finds the book a source of pleasure and commends it to all
animal lovers.

18 [SANBORN, FRANKLIN BENJAMIN.] "Emerson and His Friends in
    Concord." New England Magazine 3 (December):411-31.

Writes about Emerson, his town, home, and Concord friends, including Thoreau.

19 BLAKE, H[ARRISON] G[RAY] O[TIS]. Introduction to <u>Thoreau's Thoughts</u>. Boston: Houghton, Mifflin, pp. iii–vi.
     Blake selects the passages for this book "for the use of those who are already interested in him, and to win, if possible new admirers of what has given me so pure and unfailing a satisfaction for now more than forty years."

20 CONWAY, MONCURE DANIEL. <u>Life of Nathaniel Hawthorne</u>. London: Walter Scott, pp. 96, 165, 201, 213.
     Comments on the Hawthorne-Thoreau boat trips; the probability that Thoreau was the model for "Donatello"; a Thoreau story about "Wayside"; and the sites of the Hawthorne and Thoreau graves.

21 ELLIS, HENRY HAVELOCK. "Sketch of Thoreau." In <u>The New Spirit</u>. London: George Bell & Sons, pp. 90–99.
     Thoreau was not a naturalist or a scientific observer. He was a moralist and an artist. His records of observations are dull and poor reading. When he does come upon a good observation he never verifies it with further investigation. "His science is that of a fairly intelligent schoolboy--a counting of birds' eggs and a running after squirrels. Of the vital and organic relationships, or even of the existence of such relationships, he seems to have no perception." His writing has an excellent style that he learned from his reading of the masters. He was "in the noblest sense of the word, a cynic . . . a moralist and a preacher." He made us aware of the wildness of nature. Reprinted in Harding, 1954, pp. 91–96.

22 JONES, SAMUEL ARTHUR. Preface to Thoreau bibliography. In <u>Thoreau's Thoughts</u>. Edited by H.G.O. Blake. Boston: Houghton, Mifflin, pp. 125–46.
     Apologizes for any lack of completeness in the bibliography, stating that "it is simply a thank-offering to Thoreau's memory, from one who has been 'lifted up and strengthened' by his example. It was compiled in the hope that it might facilitate the study of, and enlarge an acquaintance with, the author of 'the only book yet written in America, to my thinking, that bears an annual perusal.'"

23 JONES, SAMUEL ARTHUR. <u>Thoreau: A Glimpse</u>. Ann Arbor, Mich.: Privately printed, 32 pp.
     Reprint of 1890.2.

24 LEIGHTON, CAROLINE C. <u>A Swiss Thoreau</u>. Boston: Lee & Shepard, 30 pp.
     Thoreau is compared to the Swiss poet and philosopher Henri Frederic Amiel.

1890

25 MABIE, HAMILTON WRIGHT. <u>Our New England</u>. Boston: Roberts
Brothers, p. 3.
Remarks on Thoreau.

26 SALT, HENRY S. Introductory note to <u>Anti-Slavery and Reform
Papers</u>. London: Swan Sonnenschein, pp. 1-20.
Lists Thoreau's published books. Notes that "the character
and opinion of Henry David Thoreau have been a stumbling-block to the
judgement of his critics." The naturalists been have baffled by his
accounts of birds and animals. Literary critics have been baffled by
his unique personality. This book sheds a new light for those who know
only <u>Walden</u> and his diaries. Refutes the claim that Thoreau was an
anarchist. "Thoreau's anarchism is, in brief, the claim for the
individual man of the right of free growth and natural development from
within—the same claim that has been advanced in other words by
Whitman, and Tolstoi, and Ibsen, and William Morris and other prophets
of democracy in the old world and the new."

27 SALT, HENRY S. <u>The Life of Henry David Thoreau</u>. London:
Bentley & Son, 315 pp.
This biography represents intensive research of all the then-
available material about Thoreau, including much correspondence with
his friends in America. It is the first biography written by one who
never met Thoreau, who could look at him objectively for the most part.
He was in agreement with much of Thoreau's philosophy and that adds
occasional bias, but not to the degree of the two previous biographies.
The first eight chapters describe Thoreau's life. The balance of
the book deals with his philosopy and his published work. A short
bibliography is appended. Revised: 1896.39.

28 WOODBURY, CHARLES J. <u>Talks with Ralph Waldo Emerson</u>. New York:
Baker & Taylor, pp. 62, 81-82.
Relates Cholmondeley's offer to pay all of Thoreau's expenses
if he would accompany him on a trip to the Amazon. Thoreau replied "I
think I had better stay in Concord." Reprint of 1890.3.

1891

1 Review of <u>Thoreau's Thoughts</u>. <u>Critic</u> 15 (24 January):42-43.
Criticizes Blake for the disjointed manner in which he uses
Thoreau's journal. States that he was not a writer of maxims
or pensées. Even his journals offer some continuity. "These
selections no more represent Thoreau than so many pailsful of water
from the Merrimac would answer for the stream." The bibliography at
the end is valuable to collectors.

2 "Notes." <u>Critic</u> 15 (7 February):78
Reports that Edward Emerson will read a paper on "The Life and

Character of Thoreau with Reminiscences" at Daniel French's studio in New York City on 16 February.

3   "Talks with Emerson." Critic 15 (28 February):105-6.
        Reviews Woodbury's Talks with Ralph Waldo Emerson. Emerson was fond of Thoreau because he enjoyed watching his development. "He had the courage of his convictions," but this author thought that Emerson meant his own convictions.

4   SALT, HENRY S. "Thoreau's Gospel of Simplicity." Paternoster Review, March.
        Salt replies completely to Lowell's objections to Thoreau and his writings.

5   "Notes." Critic 15 (23 May):282.
        Disagrees with the Boston Daily Advertiser that the best portrait of Thoreau is the weak crayon head made by Rowse in 1854; nor is the full-bearded one taken at New Bedford in 1861 the best but, rather the one taken for Blake about 1856. It pictures him in full health "as he might be seen emerging from the pine forest of Maine, or a flowering swamp in Concord--his hair copious and tossed about, his face full and a little rustic, with all its indications of deep thought, and with a thin fringe of beard on his throat, which he wore not for ornament, but to protect his throat."

6   "Thoughts." Boston Evening Post, 10 June.
        Reviews Thoreau's Thoughts and believes that his writings do much to make life better.

7   [JONES, SAMUEL ARTHUR.] "An Afternoon in the University Library." Inlander 1 (June):150-53.
        A fanciful story in which the author dreams that he was one of the copies of A Week on the Concord and Merrimack Rivers returned in sheets to Thoreau and stored in his attic room.

8   [SANBORN, FRANKLIN BENJAMIN.] "Thoreau's Love of Colors." Springfield Republican, 16 July, p. 4.
        Notes that Channing visited the 1870 hermit of Walden Pond, Hotham, and wrote a poem about the late-fall colors at Walden, and that Thoreau loved the homely colors of winter. Reprinted in Cameron, 1981a, p. 67.

9   JONES, SAMUEL ARTHUR. "Thoreau and His Biographers." Lippincott's Magazine 48 (August):224-28.
        Appraises the four biographies that have been written about Thoreau and discovers all of them wanting except Salt's, which also is occasionally marred by statements that he had received from Sanborn. Is happy that each succeeding biographer has improved on the others; Channing's book has much of the unpublished journals; Page's

1891

gives just what Thoreau's books tell, but it does whet the reader's
appetite for more; Sanborn's is full of misrepresentations and
miscellany not concerning Thoreau; Salt's new book is a labor of love
by a follower of Thoreau. Reprinted in Glick, 1969, pp. 119-25.

10 HARTE, BRET. "A Few Words about Mr. Lowell." New Review 5
     (September):193-201.
         Obituary of Lowell mentioning Thoreau.

11 [SANBORN, FRANKLIN BENJAMIN.] "Increasing Popularity of Thoreau
     / Stories About Him." Springfield Republican, 19 October, p. 4.
         Notes that young men often travel hundreds, even thousands
of miles to visit Thoreau's haunts. This is an indication of his
lasting fame. Tells of a visit by one of these youths and their talk
about stories concerning Thoreau. Reprinted in Cameron, 1981a, p. 68.

12 [SANBORN, FRANKLIN BENJAMIN.] "Samuel Rowse's Portrait of
     General Charles Lowell / His Crayons of Thoreau and Emerson."
     Springfield Republican, 26 October, p. 4.
         Relates the background of the Rowse portrait and remarks on
the Worcester and New Bedford photographs. Reprinted in Cameron,
1981a, p. 69.

13 CALDWELL, JOSHUA W. "Ten Volumes of Thoreau." New Englander 55
     (November):404-24.
         Harshly critical of all of Thoreau's books because of his
unusual philosophy.

14 HIGGINSON, THOMAS WENTWORTH. "Glimpses of Authors. IV. The
     Transcendental Authors." Brains 1 (1 December):103-6.
         Writes of the time when he asked Thoreau to lecture in Boston
and his timidity in accepting the offer.

*15 JONES, SAMUEL ARTHUR. "James Russell Lowell." Inlander 2
      (December):121-25.
          Source: Allen, p. 130.

16 "The Thoreau Club Girls." A broadside of a poem apparently
     printed between 1891 and 1894 for the members of the "Thoreau
     Club" of Leroy, N.Y.
         The theme is the meeting of Dame Nature while reading a volume
of Thoreau. Reprinted in TSB, no. 7 (Fall 1961) p. 4.

17 BOLLES, FRANK. Land of the Lingering Snow. Boston: Houghton,
     Mifflin, pp. 98, 102, 197.
         Mentions Thoreau in passing.

18 DIRCKS, WILL H., ed. Prefatory note to Essays and Other Writings
     of Henry Thoreau. London: Walter Scott, pp. vii-xv.

Mysticism was a part of Thoreau and showed in his life and writings. Transcendentalism was predominant. "The natural philosopher arrived haltingly only in the second place." He fought against gregariousness. He always expected rarer and finer than life gives but was not sure what that was.

19 ELLIOTT, WALTER. Life of Father Hecker. New York: Columbus Press, p. 140.
     Gives Isaak Hecker's impression of Thoreau's mother and her concern for him.

20 GRAHAM, P. ANDERSON. "The Philosophy of Idleness." In Nature in Books. London: Methuen, pp. 66–93.
     Reviews Thoreau's life and philosophy in light of the influences that shaped that life. Defends and approves his asceticism and condemns the early Emerson influence. "He was the most perfectly unsophisticated and natural man of his times."

*21 GROUSSAC, PAUL. En su obra Del Plata al Niagara, editada en Buenos Aires, hay un ensayo itiulado Awakening of New England en el cual a Thoreau solo por el nombre y colocado entre muchos escritores, p. 421.
     Listed in Thoreau Society Booklet, no. 24 (1970), p. 1.

22 HAWTHORNE, JULIAN, and LEONARD LEMMON. American Literature. Boston: D.C. Heath, pp. 145–48.
     Sketches Thoreau's life and philosophy. Considers him "bilious in constitution and in temper, with a disposition somewhat prone to suspicion and jealousy, and defiant, rather than truly independent, in spirit." He tried to cast off the Emerson influence and succeeded in part, but occasionaly it showed through in his writings.

23 KNORTZ, KARL. Geschichte der nordamerikanischen Litteratur. Berlin: Verlag von Hans Lustenoder, pp. 283–93.
     Notes that although Thoreau was a violent abolitionist his writings will always be among the classics of American literature.

24 ROBERTSON, JOHN M. Modern Humanists. London: Swan Sonnenschein, pp. 130–33.
     Notes that Emerson "was a magnetic and commanding personality as shown by his marked influence on Thoreau, who, however, made the Emersonian style as much his own as Emerson did when he developed it from his aunt." Thoreau showed Emerson the proper approach on the slavery question.

26 [SCUDDER, HORACE.] "Henry D. Thoreau." In Masterpieces of American Literature. Boston: Houghton, Mifflin, p. 161–65.
     Biographical sketch commenting on his philosophy and his

1891

writings. "He has a way, almost insolent, of throwing out his
thoughts, and growling forth his objections to the conventions of life,
which renders his writing often crabbed and inartistic. . . . Yet
often his indiffernce to style is a rugged insistence on the strongest
thought, and in his effort to express himself unreservedly he reaches a
force and energy which are refreshing." Reprints "Wild Apples" from
Excursions.

1892

1   SANBORN, FRANKLIN BENJAMIN. "At the Breakfast Table." Boston
    Daily Advertiser, 8 March.
        Discusses Thoreau's poems.

2   SANBORN, FRANKLIN BENJAMIN. "At the Breakfast Table." Boston
    Daily Advertiser, 18 March.
        Writes about Thoreau's reading.

3   "Boston Letter." Critic 17 (19 March):170.
        Notes that the building in Concord that Henry and John
Thoreau used for a private school has been sold to Charles Emerson.
Ellery Channing who lived in the house for some time now resides with
Franklin Sanborn.

4   "Henry D. Thoreau's Works." Truth Seeker, 26 March, p. 206.
        Believes Thoreau will become a philosophical classic author.
He was a "crank" who joined with all revolters against much of the
social order. A short biography calls him Henry Daniel Thoreau who was
skillful in wanting little. He lived and felt inspiration from India's
mystical literature. Claims that he loved nature as much as the
philosophy of India. He was a transcendentalist but not a Christian.
Notes that a new edition of his books has been released.

5   "Magazine Notes." Critic 17 (9 April):211.
        Remembers that Thoreau felt that when one walked there should
be no specified time of walking or exact end in view. Julian Hawthorne
writes in the April Lippincott's that this was a Thoreau affectation.
"It depends, we should say, on what one walks for--pleasure, or muscle,
or the gate-money."

*6   UNDERWOOD, SARA A. "Sketches of Concord Philosophers."
    Belford's Monthly 10 (April):675-88.
        Source: Undated sales catalog of G.A. Baker, New York,
listing a collection of items by or pertaining to Thoreau.

7   "Magazine Notes." Critic 17 (7 May):265.
        Reviews "The Emerson-Thoreau Correspondence" published in the

May <u>Atlantic Monthly</u>. The letters came from either Concord, where
Thoreau was living in the Emerson house, or from Staten Island, where
he was "learning to hate New York."

   8 NOE, HEINRICH. "Henry David Thoreau." <u>Beilage zur allgemeinen</u>
      <u>Zeitung</u>, no. 116 (18 May), pp. 1-5.
      Compares <u>Walden</u> with the novels of Jean Paul Richter.

   9 ADAMS, W.I. LINCOLN. "A Faithful Lover of Nature." <u>Frank</u>
      <u>Leslie's Popular Monthly</u> 33 (May):574-76.
      Thoreau's life at Walden was merely one part of his whole
career which was "consistent and harmonious." Gives a brief
biographical sketch.

  10 SANBORN, FRANKLIN BENJAMIN. "The Emerson-Thoreau Correspond-
      ence." <u>Atlantic Monthly</u> 69 (May):577-96; (June):736-53.
      Sanborn feels that many of the articles and books on Emerson
did not adequately treat the Emerson-Thoreau relationship and hopes
that the publication of their correspondence will make the public aware
of their closeness.

  11 "Magazine Notes." <u>Critic</u> 17 (25 June):352.
      Comments on the June installment of the Emerson-Thoreau
correspondence in the <u>Atlantic Monthly</u>.

  12 ALGER, WILLIAM ROUNSEVILLE. "Everyday Philosophy." <u>Boston</u>
      <u>Evening Transcript</u>, 6 August, p. 4.
      Finds Thoreau's "Battle of the Ants" from <u>Walden</u> good reading.

  13 [SANBORN, FRANKLIN BENJAMIN.] Review of <u>Autumn</u>. <u>Boston Daily</u>
      <u>Advertiser</u>, 14 September.
      Gives some anecdotes about Thoreau and his friend, Miss Mary
Emerson.

  14 B[LACKWELL], H[ENRY] B. Review of <u>Autumn</u>. <u>Boston Woman's</u>
      <u>Journal</u>, 24 September, p. 309.
      Predicts that this book will be well received by all lovers of
Thoreau's books.

  15 "Men and Nature." <u>New-York Daily Tribune</u>, 2 October, p. 14.
      Reviews <u>Autumn,</u> saying that if living with high thoughts makes
one an aristocrat, then Thoreau was one. <u>Autumn</u> is full of loving
observations of nature. Those who care for his books will look forward
to each new volume of his journals.

  16 [SANBORN, FRANKLIN BENJAMIN.] "Portion of a Lost Thoreau Letter
      on Want of Success as a Lecturer." <u>Boston Daily Advertiser</u>, 12
      October, p. 4.

1892

Prints part of a letter of 7 February 1855 to Thomas
Cholmondeley in which Thoreau says that he either walks or skates every
day and has more to do with nature than with man. Reports on the
doings of Cholmondeley's Concord acquaintances. Admits that he has had
little success as a lecturer. Complete letter is reprinted in Harding
and Bode, The Correspondence of Henry David Thoreau (New York: New
York University Press, 1958), pp. 370–72.

17 "Thoreau's Autumn." Critic 18 (26 November):292–93.
      Notes that the Emersonian touch was strong in Thoreau's
journal in 1840; by 1851 it becomes a stronger observation with even
stronger expression of thoughts, more real but still idealistic. The
change from the abstract of Emerson to the concrete is for the better.
"He saw life steadily. Can we say he saw it whole? He at least saw a
beautiful part of it clearly and amply."

18 B., P.J. Review of Autumn. Vassar Miscellany 22 (November):92–
      94.
      Does not consider this book a history of Thoreau's life but
rather a record of the changes in the autumn days, which are carefully
chronicled and should be pleasantly accepted as such.

19 ABBOTT, CHARLES C. "A Victim of Thoreau." In Recent Rambles.
      Philadelphia: J.B. Lippincott, pp. 62–69.
      Records a conversation between the author and a tramp who read
Walden thirty-five years before and tries unsuccessfully to live a life
without working.

20 BALL, BENJAMIN W. "Thoreau." In The Merrimack River, Hellenics
      and Other Poems. New York: G.P. Putnam's Sons, p. 50.
      Verse.

21 BLAKE, H[ARRISON] G[RAY] O[TIS], ed. Preface to Autumn. Boston:
      Houghton, Mifflin, pp. iii–vi.
      In this, the final volume of the seasons, the editor feels
that he has discharged his moral obligation to Thoreau for bequeathing
his journals to him. Notes that the writings show the "cheerful
serenity" of a man who was accomplishing his aim in life. He took
little part in philanthropy or reform. Had he done so his character
would have been changed.

22 BREED, GEO. J., and WM G. BARTON. "Thoreau, Flagg, and
      Burroughs." In Songs and Saunterings of a Poet and a Naturalist.
      Salem, Mass.: Salem Press & Publishing, pp. 1–17.
      Students of Thoreau's writings invariably find that they must
also study the man. Arriving at an objective conclusion is impossible
without understanding his character. Reprinted from 1885.2.

23 BURROUGHS, JOHN. "Thoreau." In Chamber's Encyclopedia. Vol.
    10. London and Edinburgh: William and Robert Chambers, pp. 184–
    85.
       Brief biographical sketch.

24 CURTIS, GEORGE WILLIAM. "Thoreau and My Lady Cavaliere." In
    From the Easy Chair. New York: Harper & Bro., pp. 62–73.
       Remarks on his first meeting with Thoreau at Emerson's house
and his following talks with him on Indians. Compares him with Daniel
Boone regarding his feelings towards the Indians.

25 HIGGINSON, THOMAS WENTWORTH. The New World and the New Book.
    Boston: Lee & Shepard, 234 pp.
       Mention of Thoreau.

26 HOLMES, OLIVER WENDELL. Ralph Waldo Emerson. American Men of
    Letters Series. Boston: Houghton, Mifflin, 441 pp.
       Calls Thoreau "the Robinson Crusoe of Walden Pond who carried
out a school-boy whim to its full proportions, and told the story of
Nature as only one who had hidden in her bedroom could have told it"
(p. 72). Feels that some traits in Thoreau can be traced to his
ancestors.

27 YEATS, WILLIAM BUTLER. "The Lake Isle of Innisfree." In The
    Countess Kathleen and Various Legends and Lyrics. London:
    Fisher Unwin.
       Reprint of 1890.15.

                              1893

1   JONES, SAMUEL ARTHUR. "Thoreau's Inheritance." Inlander 3
    (February):199–204.
       An important factor of Thoreau's inheritance was his endow-
ment of heredity, which the biographers have not yet fully considered.
Reprinted in Jones, Thoreau: A Glimpse (Concord, Mass.: Erudite
Press, 1903), viii, 35 pp.

2   [SANBORN, FRANKLIN BENJAMIN.] "The Breakfast Table." Boston
    Daily Advertiser, 15 March.
       Prints extracts from Channing's out-of-print Thoreau.

3   "Editor's Chair." New England Magazine, n.s. 8 (March):132.
       Reviews Thoreau's Cape Cod, noting that his picture is one-
sided for he did not go to the inland country.

4   [HOSMER, HORACE R.] "Reminiscences of Thoreau." Concord
    Enterprise, 22 April.

1893

Comments on seeing Thoreau's pleasure at discovering a climbing fern.

5 [HOSMER, HORACE R.]. "Reminiscences of Thoreau." Concord Enterprise, 15 May.
   Recounts some incidents in Thoreau's life.

6 "Famous Old Landmarks." Boston Globe, 16 May.
   Description the Boston house owned by Thoreau's grandfather, John Thoreau, with a picture of the house. Reports that it is being razed.

7 [MACDONALD, E.M.] "An Ideal for Free Thinkers. Truth Seeker, 24 June, pp. 387–88.
   Considers Thoreau to be a man of strict integrity and high morality. Quotes his friend Ellery Channing, calling him William Henry Channing. Notes that he was one of the earliest protesters against slavery. Considers him a Natural Man, in contrast to the artificial product of his day. "He spurned Christianity, the Religion of Sorrow, . . . mentally affiliated himself with the glad and free paganisms of antiquity whose creeed was enjoyment and pride." Concludes with "What a world this would be were all—men, women and children—of the strain of Thoreau. Excellent Thoreau, independent, tranquil, bountiful, feeling, truth-telling, honest, sage, undauntable, free—when shall we be like thee?"

8 "New Publications / Henry David Thoreau." Truth Seeker, 24 June, p. 398.
   Reviews the book, listing and commenting on the different chapters. Considers the biography a satisfactoy one. Notes that an anaylsis of Thoreau's character is given on the editorial pages of the same issue.

9 NEWTON-ROBERTSON, JANETTA. Review of Stevenson's Men and Books. Westminster Review, July.
   Notes that Thoreau left his mark on Stevenson although at first there might appear little sympathy between Thoreau, "the ungenial philosopher of the economy of life," and Stevenson, "a herald of gospel of Joy." Reprinted in part: Critic 20 (5 August):94.

10 "Thoreau." Belgravia 81 (August):375–83.
   Appreciates Thoreau's love for nature.

11 [SANBORN, FRANKLIN BENJAMIN.] "The Works of Thoreau about to Be Issued / Observations on a Week / Some Textual Corrections." Springfield Republican, 28 October, p. 9.
   Comments on the first two volumes of the Riverside Edition and points out errors. Notes that Theodore Parker wrote on the margin of

his _Dial_, next to the Thoreau poem "The Gentle Boy," that "This boy is a girl." Reprinted in Cameron, 1981a, p. 73.

12 Announcement of Thoreau reprints. _Nation_ 57 (2 November):328.
    Notes the publication of the ten volumes of the Riverside Edition of Thoreau's works.

13 [SANBORN, FRANKLIN BENJAMIN.] "The New Edition of _Cape Cod_ / Thoreau's Approach to His Subject." _Springfield Republican_, 4 November, p. 9.
    Remarks that there was some resentment by the inhabitants on the Cape after the magazine publication of sections of Thoreau's _Cape Cod_. It was felt that he was making fun of them. Reprinted in Cameron, 1981a, p. 73.

14 [SANBORN, FRANKLIN BENJAMIN.] "Thoreau in England / The Cholmondeley Correspondence." _Springfield Republican_, 2 December, p. 2.
    Repeats the comments of an English student that "there seems to be little commercial interest in Thoreau's books here. Had he written the usual literary tittle-tattle and balderdash, he would have thousands of readers. He will have to wait a half a century or so, to give time for a few bubble reputations to vanish." Reprinted Cameron, 1981a, p. 74.

15 "Thoreau's English Crony." _Critic_ 20 (9 December):375.
    Reviews the December _Atlantic Monthly_, noting the Sanborn article on Thoreau and his English friend Thomas Chomondeley.

16 "The Riverside Thoreau." _Boston Herald_, 18 December.
    Comments on the new editions of Thoreau's books and remarks that Thoreau and Emerson borrowed nothing from each other but both were inspired by the same source. Says that with this first complete set of his works, Thoreau has taken a place in the front rank of American authors.

17 ANGELL, GEORGE T. _Our Dumb Animals_, December.
    Briefly appreciates Thoreau's love for nature.

18 SANBORN, F[RANKLIN] B[ENJAMIN]. "Thoreau and His English Friend Thomas Chomondeley." _Atlantic Monthly_ 72 (December):741-56.
    Describes how the two men met and were attracted to each other because of their similar interests. Quotes from their correspondence.

*19 TREVOR, JOHN. "Thoreau." _Labour Prophet_ 2 (December):190.
    Cited in Allen, _A Bibliography of Henry David Thoreau_, p. 131.

1893

20 HORTON, EDWARD A. Noble Lives and Noble Deeds. Boston:
    Unitarian Sunday-School Society, pp. 103-8.
        A Sunday school lesson on nature, relating it to Thoreau's
philosophy, life, works, and fame.

21 HUDSON, W[ILLIAM] H[ENRY]. Birds in a Village. London: Chapman
    & Hall, pp. 153, 190.
        Thinks that a certain bird note made him sad that there were
no cocks to break the solitude of Walden. Considers Walden should be
listed with books with love of nature.

22 JAPP, ALEXANDER H[AY]. Hours in My Garden. New York:
    Macmillan, p. 171.
        Comments on Thoreau's observations on the bird, nightjar.

23 NUMQUAM [ROBERT BLATCHFORD]. Merrie England. London: Clarion
    Press, pp. 17, 93-95.
        One of a series of letters on the English labor problems
addressed to an imaginary John Smith advising him to read Walden.
Quotes extracts from the writings of prominent men, including Thoreau,
to prove that socialists are not insignificant. Includes Walden in a
list of books to be read by socialists. Reviewed in TSB, no. 98
(Winter 1967), pp. 1-3.

24 SALT, HENRY S. Richard Jefferies: A Study. London: Swan
    Sonnenschein, 128 pp.
        Thoreau set out on a life-long pursuit of nature. Jefferies,
like Thoreau, was unaware in his youth of the influence nature was to
play in his life.

25 SANBORN, FRANKLIN BENJAMIN, and WILLIAM T. HARRIS. A. Bronson
    Alcott: His Life and Philosophy. 2 vols. Boston: Roberts
    Brothers, 679 pp.
        Notes that Thoreau assisted Emerson in editing the Dial.
A year after Alcott returned to Concord after his unsuccessful
Fruitlands experiment Thoreau went to Walden Pond to establish his own
"community of one" (2:427). Gives many Thoreau quotations.

26 STONE, HERBERT STUART. First Editions of American Authors.
    Cambridge: Stone & Kimball, pp. 195-96.
        Lists Thoreau's book publications.

27 TRIGGS, OSCAR LOVELL. Browning and Whitman: A Study in
    Democracy. London: Swan Sonnenschein, pp. 34-37.
        Considers Emerson and Thoreau as literary exponents of the
revolutionary war, which was fought for individual freedom. Thoreau
was an uncompromising individual who felt that complete freedom should
be given to an individual for the expression of his character along
natural lines. He was against the formation of social colonies like

the Brook Farm experiment and knew that they could not succeed because they suppressed the individual.

28 UNDERWOOD, FRANCIS. <u>The Builders of America</u>. 1st ser. Boston: Lee & Shepard, pp. 213-16.
     Gives a brief biography of Thoreau. Calls him one of the first nihilists, repudiating any allegiance to a church, a state, or society. His books contain "sharp railings against the existing order of things" as well as studies of nature and the philosphers and poets. His books, however, do show the beauty of nature around Concord, but nowhere does he show sympathy for his fellow men. His writings show "a trace of irritation at the thought of having been so indebted to Emerson." He did not wish to be considered an Emerson disciple. States that he never shook hands nor did he ever help anyone in need.

29 WHITE, JAMES T., ed. "Henry David Thoreau." In <u>National Cyclopedia of American Biography</u>, 2:300-301.
     Considers Thoreau as a pessimist who had a "lofty scorn" for men and their traditions, but he did love nature, had high literary quality, and was a fine scholar.

1894

1 [SANBORN, FRANKLIN BENJAMIN.] "Thoreau's Style--Latest Grouping of His Works." <u>Springfield Republican</u>, 6 January, p. 9.
     Briefly reviews the final volumes of Thoreau's collected works. Reprinted in Cameron, 1981a, p. 75.

2 [SANBORN, FRANKLIN BENJAMIN.] "A New Gathering of Thoreau's Writings." <u>Springfield Republican</u>, 10 February, p. 3.
     Reviews <u>Familiar Letters</u>, saying that it shows him "in more sportive and even trivial moods than those grave essays in the epistolary form, selected by Mr. Emerson 29 years ago." Reprinted in Cameron, 1981a, p. 77.

3 ALLEN, IRVING. "Of the Thoreaus." <u>Boston Daily Advertiser</u>, 23 April.
     Recollections of the Thoreau family, noting that Henry found any social gathering exceedingly distasteful and that the people of Concord found him shy and eccentric.

*4 SANBORN, F[RANKLIN] B[ENJAMIN]. "Mr Sanborn Corrects Mr Allen." <u>Boston Daily Advertiser</u>, 25 April.
     Source: Allen, p. 132.

1894

  *5 ALLEN, IRVING. "Mr. Allen's Retort Courteous." <u>Boston Daily
      Advertiser</u>, 3 May.
        Source: Allen, p. 132.

   6 LOOMIS, E[BEN] J[ENKS]. "The Thoreaus." <u>Boston Daily
      Advertiser</u>, 8 May.
        Writes, in a letter to the editor, of his visit in 1876 to
  Sleepy Hollow Cemetery at Concord at the same time that Thoreau's
  sister, Sophia, was buried.

   7 [SANBORN, FRANKLIN BENJAMIN.] "Basilides The Gnostic / Discussed
      in One of Cholmondeley's Gifts to Thoreau / Thoreau's
      Epigrammatic Style." <u>Springfield Republican</u>, 26 May, p. 2.
        Relates the story of Basilides. Announces that the
  publication of the volume of Thoreau's letters scheduled for 26 May has
  been delayed until June because of "exigencies of the index." It will
  have some five hundred pages, nearly double the number of the 1865
  edition. Reprinted in Cameron, 1981a, p. 80.

   8 [SANBORN, FRANKLIN BENJAMIN.] "Inadequacy of Henry Nourse's
      [Town History] on the Alcott-Lane Fruitlands." <u>Springfield
      Republican</u>, 23 June, p. 8.
        Corrects Nourse's statement that Thoreau was a visitor to
  Fruitlands in 1843 by noting that the new volume of letters shows that
  he was staying with the William Emerson family at Staten Island that
  year. Reprinted in Cameron, 1981a, p. 81.

   9 [SANBORN, FRANKLIN BENJAMIN.] "Tracing Thoreau's Experiences at
      Mt. Greylock--The Hidden Record Concerning Thoreau in the
      Berkshire Hills." <u>Springfield Republican</u>, 30 June, p. 8.
        Presents a case to show that Thoreau meant Mt. Greylock when
  he wrote "Housack Mountain" in <u>A Week on the Concord and Merrimack
  Rivers</u> (Riverside Edition), p. 235. Reprinted in Cameron, 1981a, p.
  81.

  10 [SANBORN, FRANKLIN BENJAMIN.] "Discovery of an Oil Painting of
      John Thoreau at the Concord Antiquarian Museum / Resemblances
      between Henry and John." <u>Springfield Republican</u>, 7 July, p. 8.
        The unsigned painting is thought to be the work of Onthank, a
  Boston painter. Reprinted in Cameron, 1981a, p. 82.

  11 [SANBORN, FRANKLIN BENJAMIN.] "Emerson, Thoreau, and the
      Transcendentalists Were Not Egotists but Free and Healthy
      People." <u>Springfield Republican</u>, 14 July, p. 8.
        Refutes the statement that Thoreau's writings display conceit
  by quoting others who feel that individuals with originality often seem
  egotistical. Reprinted in Cameron, 1981a, p. 82.

12 [SANBORN, FRANKLIN BENJAMIN.] "Limitations of Howells after
    Thirty-five Years / His Blindspot for Thoreau and Others."
    Springfield Republican, 28 July, p. 8.
        Does not feel that Howells has reached "the serene spaces of
literature" to enable him to wisely judge Thoreau and other Concord
poets. Reprinted in Cameron, 1981a, p. 83.

13 "Notes." Critic 22 (25 August):128.
        Reports that Edward Emerson will give a lecture entitled "The
Story of Thoreau's Life" at South Place Chapel, Finsbury, London, on
the last Sunday of September.

14 HOWELLS, WILLIAM DEAN. "My First Visit to New England, Fourth
    Part." Harper's Monthly Magazine 89 (August):441–51.
        Recounts his first meeting with Thoreau, who seemed to remain
in a dreamy muse and repulsed all attempts at conversation.

15 "Momento of John Thoreau & Son, Pencil Manufacturers." Boston
    Herald, 6 September.
        Describes the Thoreau pencils and the various finds of them.

16 [SANBORN, FRANKLIN BENJAMIN.] "Edward Emerson's Lectures in
    London on Thoreau and on John Sterling's Correspondence with
    R.W.E." Springfield Republican, 8 September, p. 8.
        Reports the Emerson lecture at the South Place Chapel in
London on Henry Thoreau, Concord schoolmaster and artisan. Reprinted
in Cameron, 1981a, p. 83.

17 Review of Familiar Letters. Critic 22 (22 September):190.
        Notes that this editor of Thoreau's letters shows a more
cheerful man than the previous edition by Emerson. Here the letters
reveal a chatty mood in which there are jokes as well as puns.

18 "New Publications / Familiar Letters of Thoreau, Edited by F.B.
    Sanborn." Boston Herald, 1 October.
        Notes that when Emerson edited Thoreau's letters he did not
use many letters that are now used in this volume because they were
considered too personal or trivial. The inclusion of these letters
gives a new dimension to Thoreau, one that cannot be found in his
formal writings.

19 BLOCK, LOUIS J. "Thoreau's Letters." Dial 17 (16 October):228–
    30.
        "The letters presented in this selection show Thoreau from his
gentlest and most familiar side. They are domestic and gossipy, they
display his simple likes and dislikes."

20 Review of Familiar Letters of Henry David Thoreau. Nation 59 (18
    October):291–92.

1894

Shows that the quantity of letters is much greater than in the 1865 edition; this one has over twice the number of pages. It contains much editorial matter giving the biographer's personal recollections. Shows Thoreau as less stoical than the earlier volume of letters edited by Emerson. Notes that Thoreau's sister objected to the letters that Emerson chose as not being typical. The early letters to Emerson copy the Emersoniam style, but the later ones are written more simply.

21 LATHROP, GEORGE PARSONS. "Report of Lathrop Lecture at the
    Brooklyn Institute." Brooklyn Citizen, 12 December.
    The speaker recalls Hawthorne's daughter's description of Thoreau flitting "in and out of the house with long, ungainly, Indian-like stride, and his piercing large orbs staring, as it were in vacancy."

22 LATHROP, GEORGE PARSONS. "On Thoreau." Brooklyn Standard Union,
    19 December.
    Gives a detailed report of the Thoreau lecture.

23 STEWART, GEORGE. "Henry David Thoreau." Canadian Magazine 4
    (December):101-9.
    Recalls an article he wrote in 1877 (see 1877.2) denouncing Thoreau, for which was reprimanded by Emerson. Prints part of Emerson's letter to him. Four years later Blake began to publish the season books. These and other Thoreau writings changed Stewart's evaluation of Thoreau. Now he admits that Thoreau will always have a place in American literature. Gives a detailed sketch of his life, with comments about his writings.

24 JONES, SAMUEL ARTHUR. "Thoreau and His Works." Inlander 4
    (1894):234-40.
    Reviews with approval the Riverside Edition of Thoreau's writings.

25 BURROUGHS, JOHN. Riverby. Boston and New York: Houghton,
    Mifflin, pp. 224-26.
    States that there is observation in Walden but the journals of Thoreau that have been published contain little worth noting. Wonders why there are so few real observations of nature in them considering that he spent much of his life spying on her ways.

26 CARY, EDWARD. George William Curtis. American Men of Letters
    Series. Boston: Houghton, Mifflin, p. 31.
    Repeats Curtis's appellation of Thoreau as "the honorable member for Blackberry Pastures."

27 CODMAN, JOHN THOMAS. Brook Farm: Historic and Personal
    Memories. Boston: Arena Publishing, pp. 6-7.

Traces the history of the Brook Farm. Notes that not one
of the original Transcendental Club joined the Ripley movement. Notes
that Thoreau spent two years in a hut in Walden Woods.

28 JONES, SAMUEL ARTHUR. <u>Bibliography of Henry David Thoreau</u>. New
York: DeVinne Press, 80 pp.
Printed for the Rowfant Club. It contains a chronology of
Thoreau's life, reviews and criticisms of his works as well as a
bibliography.

29 NORTON, CHARLES ELIOT, ed. <u>Letters of James Russell Lowell</u>. 2
vols. New York: Harper & Brothers, 1:27.
Notes that Lowell met Thoreau one night and was amused to
see how he imitated Emerson in tone and manner.

30 PICKARD, SAMUEL T., ed. <u>Life and Letters of John Greenleaf
Whittier</u>. 2 vols. Boston: Houghton, Mifflin, 1:359.
Notes Whittier's comment on reading <u>Walden</u>: "capital reading
but very wicked and heathenish."

31 RUTHERFORD, MILDRED. "Henry David Thoreau." In <u>American
Authors</u>. Atlanta: Franklin Printing, pp. 297–301.
Comments on the various characteristics of Thoreau's family.
Says that Thoreau's mother loved to wear bright colors and was once
reproved by Emerson's aunt for this weakness. She was eighty-four at
the time, and Mrs. Thoreau was seventy. John Thoreau, Henry's father,
was a silent man who "led a quiet, plodding, unambitious life." Notes
an eccentric Uncle Charles who was a nonprofessional juggler and
jester. Gives a short biography of Thoreau noting at the conclusion
that he was spoken of as a failure, but as time goes on "the dross is
melting from his writings and the gold is seen."

32 SALT, HENRY S. <u>Animal Rights</u>. New York and London: Macmillan,
pp. 28, 31–32, 52, 73.
Quotes from Thoreau's writings to show that animals have a
vital spirit or <u>anima</u> and it is as wrong to kill and eat them as it was
for the cannibals to eat each other.

33 SANBORN, F[RANKLIN] B[ENJAMIN], ed. Introduction to <u>Familiar
Letters of Henry David Thoreau</u>. Cambridge: Houghton, Mifflin,
pp. v–xii.
Shows with statements by Thoreau's friends that he was a much
kinder and friendlier person than the 1865 edition of his letters would
imply. Wishes these letters, which have been chosen to illustrate his
domestic and gossipy moods, to convey a better balanced Thoreau.

34 [SCUDDER, HORACE ELISHA.] Introductory note to <u>Cape Cod</u>.
Boston: Houghton, Mifflin, p. [v].
Notes the publishing background of sections of this book.

1894

35 [SCUDDER, HORACE ELISHA.] Introductory note to Excursions.
    Boston: Houghton, Mifflin, pp. vii–x.
        Notes that "A Yankee in Canada," which was originally printed
with Anti-Slavery and Reform Papers in a separate volume, is here the
first sketch. Reviews the other articles in the book.

36 [SCUDDER, HORACE ELISHA.] Introductory note to The Maine Woods.
    Boston: Houghton, Mifflin, pp. vii–x.
        Reviews Thoreau's trips to Maine that made up the book.
Relates the previous publications of sections.

37 [SCUDDER, HORACE ELISHA.] Introductory note to Miscellanies.
    Boston: Houghton, Mifflin, pp. vii–xi.
        Notes the history of the gathering of the fugitive articles
used in this book and the problems with the magazine publishing of some
of the essays.

38 [SCUDDER, HORACE ELISHA.] Introductory note to Walden. Boston:
    Houghton, Mifflin, pp. vii–viii.
        "The life in the woods was a characteristic expression of his
stout independence of conditions, and served his purpose of living
frugally and securing leisure for observation, reading, and writing.
But since the act was in a way unique, it transferred something of its
unique property to the book which recorded it, and the book is more
closely identified with Thoreau's fame, has done more to give him
distinction, than any other of his writings."

39 [SCUDDER, HORACE ELISHA.] Introductory note to A Week on the
    Concord and Merrimack Rivers. Boston: Houghton, Mifflin, pp.
    ix–xvii.
        Relates the history of the making of the book mentioning that
it includes many poems first printed in the Dial. After many fruitless
attempts to find a publisher, Thoreau decided to have it published at
his own expense. Quotes from reviews of the book by Ripley and Lowell.
The book did not sell well, and seven hundred and six unsold copies
were returned to Thoreau in 1853.

40 SMITH, BENJAMIN E. The Century Cyclopedia of Names. New York:
    Century, p. 993.
        Short biographical sketch.

41 WATKINS, MILDRED CABELL. American Literature. New York:
    American Book Co., p. 73.
        States that Thoreau was as eccentric as Alcott. He went to
Walden Pond, where he lived for two years on $68.76. He despised
society and civilization. At times he would go to Maine and live for
several weeks with the Indians.

42 WHITCOMB, SELDON L. <u>Chronological Outlines of American</u>
    <u>Literature</u>. New York: Macmillan, pp. 79, 164, 170, 180,
    182, 202, 278
        Lists all of Thoreau books chronologically with publications
of other authors for the same year.

1895

1 [JUPP, W.J.?] "The Poet-Naturalists / Henry David Thoreau."
   <u>Great Thoughts</u> (London), 19 January, pp. 256–58; 26 January, pp.
   268–87.
        Regards Wordsworth as the finest nature poet and Darwin as the
greatest naturalist but considers Ellery Channing correct in calling
Thoreau the first "Poet-Naturalist" because he combined the qualities
of nature's beauty with the study of nature. Notes Thoreau's parentage
and life as well as his devotion to nature. Considers <u>Walden</u> to be a
sincere autobiography to be ranked with Wordsworth's "Prelude" and the
"Confessions" of Rousseau and Augustine. Admits that he had
limitations, such as his egotism. Prints a new portrait of Thoreau.
Incorrectly states that he died at the age of fifty-five.

2 JONES, SAMUEL ARTHUR. "A Belated Knight-Errant." <u>Inlander</u> 5
   (February).
        Recalls George William Curtis's outings with Thoreau.

3 SANBORN, F[RANKLIN] B[ENJAMIN]. "Thoreau's <u>Poems of Nature</u>."
   <u>Scribner's Magazine</u> 17 (March):325–55.
        Prints a letter of 11 March 1842 from Thoreau to Emerson,
written soon after the deaths of young Waldo Emerson, Ralph Waldo
Emerson's son, and John Thoreau, Henry's brother. Reprints some
Thoreau poetry, with comments.

4 LEWIN, WALTER. Review of Salt's <u>Selections from Thoreau</u>.
   <u>Academy</u> 47 (4 May):377.
        Reviews the book with approval and shows appreciation for
Thoreau as a person. Considers the selections judiciously picked and
discusses each.

5 Review of 1895.6. <u>Critic</u> 23 (8 June):420.
        Although the paper is short, Thoreau admirers will receive it
with pleasure, as will all lovers of nature. Reprinted in <u>TSB</u>, no. 133
(Fall 1975), pp. 5–6.

6 ABBOTT, CHARLES. "Thoreau." <u>Lippincott's Monthly Magazine</u> 55
   (June):852–55.
        Refutes Lowell's article (1865.22) and Emerson's obituary
(1862.3), using facts to prove his case. Believes that Thoreau's

1895

influence will last as long as the English language. Reprinted in
Glick, 1969, pp. 125-30.

7   B[LACKWELL], H[ENRY] B. Review of Thoreau's Familiar Letters.
    Boston Woman's Journal, 6 July, p. 211.
        Finds the contents of this book "delightful."

8   ALLEN, IRVING. "American Women to Whom the World is Indebted."
    Independent 47 (25 July):987-88.
        Comments on Thoreau's mother and his sister, Sophia.

9   HOSMER, ALFRED. "Anent Thoreau." Natural Food (Surrey,
    England), July.
        Corrects an error in 1895.10 in a letter to the editor.

10 WAYLEN, HECTOR. "A Visit of Walden Pond." Natural Food (Surry,
    England), July.
        Relates a story about Thoreau told by George Bartlett.
Describes the wooden picnic sheds that have sprung up at one end of
Walden Pond. Reprinted in TSB, no. 69 (Fall 1959), p. [2].

11 "Thoreau's Trout in the Milk." Critic 24 (28 September):205.
        Notes that a Mr. Hyde, in an article in the 24 August Critic
on 'The Dignity of the Teacher,' refers to Sherlock Holmes's statement:
"Circumstantial evidence is convincing as when you find a trout in the
milk" and says that it should read Henry D. Thoreau instead of Holmes.
Mr. Hyde defends his statement, saying that in the book referred to,
Holmes did qualify the statement, adding "to quote Thoreau's example";
but in this case abridgment was necessary. Reprinted in TSB, no. 133
(Fall 1975), p. 6.

12 [SANBORN, FRANKLIN BENJAMIN.] "The Publication of Thoreau's
    Poems." Springfield Republican, 3 October, p. 10.
        Reviews Poems of Nature, noting that Salt's introduction
states "there is a frank and unpretending nobleness in many of
Thoreau's verses, distinguished as they are, at their very best, by
their rich fullness of thought, quiet gravity of tone, and
epigrammatical terseness of expression." Reprinted in Cameron, 1981a,
p. 89.

13 TRYON, KATE. "A Day Afield." Boston Daily Advertiser, 15
    October, p. 5.
        Reviews a lecture, "David Henry Thoreau," by Mrs. Tryon, in
which she considers Thoreauism to mean a desire to go away from society
for a while and live with nature to regain perspective on life.

14 "Reminiscences of Thoreau." Boston Daily Globe, 26 October.
        Notes the meeting on Thoreau at the French studio.

15 "A Thoreau Group." <u>Boston Daily Advertiser</u>, 26 October.
      Reports that a group of about sixty persons gathered in Daniel
French's studio to hear Alfred Hosmer talk about Thoreau. Others,
including Frank Sanborn and Walton Ricketson, spoke briefly.

16 W[ARREN], I[NA] R[USELLE]. "Henry David Thoreau." <u>Magazine of
      Poetry</u> 7 (October):421.
      Comments on his poetry,saying that he "had simplified life
till he had realized the fine savage in himself."

17 "Thoreau as a Poet." <u>London Daily Chronicle</u>, 9 November, p. 3.
      Reviews <u>Poems of Nature</u>. Considers that America produced two
famous prose writers in the early Victorian days, Emerson and Thoreau,
but "each faced in opposite directions." Thoreau wrote with a stately
grace; Emerson was "staider and more severe." Thoreau's subject matter
gives him more popularity. Notes that Thoreau burned much of his
poetry at the urging of Emerson. There is "very little art in his
poetry, [his] rhymes [are] paltry [and his] metres wanting in melody."
He was reflective like Wordsworth but "his blood never tingled in his
thoughts as it tingled in Wordsworth." His poetry is that of Quarles
and Herbert. Believes that Thoreau is too rigid a Puritan in his
poetry to forget himself; "Or perhaps it was that he could never lose
himself. It must be pitiful to feel that you could, and know that you
can't." Abandoned poetry in 1843 to the benefit of all but in view of
his other accomplishments "to apologise for his weakness would be a
piece of impertinence."

18 "An Evening with Thoreau." <u>Concord High School Voice</u>, 15
      November.
      Staples tells in his own words how Thoreau did not want to
leave the jail after his fine had been paid.

19 "The Lounger." <u>Critic</u> 27 (30 November):371.
      Comments on the magazine <u>Yellow Book</u>, noting that the term
yellowness as an objectionable feature must have been around when
Thoreau wrote in <u>A Week</u>: "The New Testament is an invaluable book,
though I must confess to having been slightly prejudiced against it in
my very early days by the church and Sabbath-School, so that it seemed,
before I read it, to be the <u>yellowest book</u> in the catalogue."

20 E[DWARDS], K[ATE] L. "Concord Letter." <u>Southbridge</u> (Mass.)
      <u>Journal</u>, 5 December, p. 2.
      Reports on the readings on Thoreau held on 28 November at
Daniel French's studio. The group was gathered by Kate Tryon.

21 WARD, ANNIE J. "Transcendental Wild Oats." <u>Springfield
      Republican</u>, 15 December, p. 5.

1895

Prints Mrs. Bronson Alcott's letters with reference to
Thoreau's mother. Reprinted in Concord Saunterer, no. 2 (Summer 1979),
pp. 23–24.

22 TRYON, KATE. "Of High Places about the Historic Town of
   Concord." Boston Daily Advertiser, 18 December, p. 8.
   Describes the exact locations of Thoreau's haunts.

23 "Poetry and Verse." Critic 24 (21 December):426.
   Reviews Poems of Nature: "Thoreau as a poet was not
only no artist, but much addicted to cocetti, a fashion which he
probably picked up from injudicious reading of the Elizabethans. His
sins of this sort count for more than Whitman's, and he has less that
is strong and original than either Whitman or Emerson, both of whom
could sing on occasion. Still there is much thought in his few
poetical pieces that is worthy of preservation."

24 ROBBINS, H. HAYES. "Concord and Those Who Have Made It Famous."
   Unitarian 10 (December):538–43.
   Brief general comments on Thoreau.

25 ABBOTT, CHARLES CONRAD. The Birds About Us. Philadelphia:
   J.B. Lippincott, p. 38.
   Quotes Thoreau's journal on certain birds.

26 ALLEN, JAMES LANE. A Kentucky Cardinal. New York: Harper &
   Brothers, pp. 66–67.
   Kentucky novel of the 1850s in which one character calls
Thoreau "the young Audubon of the Maine woods," whose writings are "as
pure and cold and lonely as a wild cedar of the mountain rocks."

27 CARPENTER, EDWARD. England's Ideal. London: Swan Sonnenschein,
   pp. 1–22.
   Comments for several pages on the decadence of modern social
life and concludes that Thoreau's philosophy of the simple life is an
ideal one for all to adopt. It is attainable through true education.

28 ELLWANGER, GEORGE H. "The Sphere of Thoreau." In Idyllists of
   the Country-Side. New York: Dodd, Mead, pp. 173–218.
   Decides that Jefferies and Thoreau are opposites, Thoreau
being picturesque and primitive while Jefferies is sympathetic and
human. The terms "prig" and "skulker" do not apply to Thoreau. Finds
it difficult to decide which of Thoreau's books reveal him best.

29 HOSMER, ALFRED W. Chronology of the Life Of Henry D. Thoreau.
   Concord, Mass.: Alfred Hosmer, 4 pp.
   Lists the important dates of Thoreau's life and his major
publications. Contains a photograph of Thoreau.

30 HUBBARD, ELBERT. <u>Little Journeys to the Homes of Good Men and</u>
   <u>Great: John Ruskin</u>. February, no. 3. New York: G.P. Putnam's
   Sons, p. 63.
      Reports on a conversation with an old man at an inn by
Coniston Water at the English Lake District, to whom he said that
Thoreau introduced Ruskin to America and that Concord was the first in
the new world to recognize him. The old gentleman said there were only
two men of genius produced in America--Thoreau and Whitman.

31 KEYSOR, JENNIE ELLIS. "Henry David Thoreau." In <u>Sketches of</u>
   <u>American Authors</u>. Boston: Educational Publishing, pp. 5-19.
      Comments on Thoreau's works and his character, together with a
biographical sketch.

32 MACDONALD, GEORGE. <u>Lilith / A Romance</u>. London: Allen & Unwin.
      Introduces this mystical novel with a passage from "Walking"
in which Thoreau does a bit of mystical thinking. Reprinted in
<u>Phantastes and Lilith</u> (Grand Rapids, Mich.: Wm. B. Eerdmans, 1964),
420 pp.

33 PRINZINGER, d[er] J[UNGER]. <u>Henry D. Thoreau, ein amerikanscher</u>
   <u>Naturschilderer</u>. Salzburg: H. Dieter f.s. Hosbuchhandler, 16
   pp.
      Monograph discussing Thoreau's relation to nature. Considers
that his greatest value lies in his reverence towards nature.

34 SALT, HENRY S., and FRANKLIN BENJAMIN SANBORN, eds. Introduction
   to <u>Poems of Nature</u>. London: John Lane; Boston and New York:
   Houghton, Mifflin, pp. xi-xix.
      Gives a critical assessment of Thoreau's poetical nature and
his ability to express it. Sums up with Thoreau's own words:

      "My life is a poem I would have writ,
      But I could not both live and utter it."

35 SALT, HENRY S., ed. Introduction to <u>Selections from Thoreau</u>.
   London: Macmillan, pp. v-xx.
      Defends Thoreau against his damaging critics, Lowell and
others. States that the best parts of his mother's character have
never been given.

36 STEARNS, FRANK PRESTON. <u>Sketches from Concord and Appledore</u>.
   New York: G.P. Putnam's Sons, 276 pp.
      Notes Thoreau's Concord life.

37 SWANN, H[ARRY] K[IRKE]. "H.D. Thoreau." In <u>Nature in Arcadia</u>.
   London: John Bale & Sons, pp. vii-viii.
      Thoreau memorial poem at the beginning of the text.

1895

38 WOLFE, THEODORE F. "The Walden of Thoreau." In Literary
    Shrines. Philadelphia: J.B. Lippincott, pp. 68–74.
        Describes a visit to the Walden Pond area, saying that Thoreau
would not know the place now for his young pines have grown tall.
Remembers Thoreau's friends and notes that today's visitors come from
afar to see the shrine.

1896

1 LE GALLIENNE, RICHARD. Review of Poems of Nature. London Star,
   23 January, p. 1.
       Thoreau moves in poetry "like a captive, with a rattle of
chains." Prose is his forte, and although he wrote that he could not
live a life and write poetry about it, he tried. His poetry is not
good; some is like Emerson's, "being poetic epigrams, gnomic
compressions of philosophy." The book will be "of interest to those
who value the greater poetry of his prose."

2 HOSMER, ALFRED W. "An Evening with Thoreau." Seed-Time
   (London), (January).
       Reports on the Concord gathering of October 1895 at Daniel
French's studio to reminisce about Thoreau.

3 "Thoreau's Verses." Saturday Review 81 (January):55.
       Reviews Poems of Nature, stating that with all of his poetical
imperfections it is not possible to take him seriously as a poet.

4 WRIGHT, M.B. "Thoreau's Uncle Peter." Boston Evening
   Transcript, 8 February.
       Recounts the history of Thoreau's great uncle Peter, who
remained on the island of Jersey when his brother sailed for America.

5 RENA, S.E. "Thoreau's Voice." Boston Evening Transcript, 15
   February, p. 15.
       In a letter to the editor, comments on a question raised in
1896.4 concerning whether or not Thoreau had retained any island music
in his voice. Confirms that in his earlier years he had a pleasant
singing voice but that after his brother's death he stopped singing.
His reading voice had a musical quality and perhaps helped him to
imitate many bird calls.

6 H., W.J. "Thoreau or Emerson." Critic 25 (4 April):235.
       In a letter to the editor, notes that the essay "Prayers"
in A Yankee in Canada is the same as in vol. 12 of the Riverside
Edition of Emerson's works. He believes the essay to be Emerson's and
wonders why the editor did not correct this error.

7 "The Lounger." Critic 25 (18 April):275.
     Commenting on an interview with novelist Herman Sudermann in
Berlin on modern English and American authors, notes that he said he
knew little of American literature. Whitman, Hawthorne, and Thoreau he
did not know at all.

8 THE TAVERNER [Edwin M. Bacon?]. "Here in Boston." Time and the
     Hour 1 (18 April):3–4.
     Recalls a military encampment at Concord when one of the
militiamen climbed a hill with Thoreau to see the inspiring scene.
After viewing it for a while Thoreau said, "Mr-----. did it ever occur
to you what a small place in Nature a camp fills?" Reprinted in part
in TSB, no. 38 (Winter 1952), pp. 3.

9 [SANBORN, FRANKLIN BENJAMIN.] "May-Day Pilgrimage to Concord /
     Letter from Henry Salt / Program at the Thoreau House."
     Springfield Republican, 2 May, p. 12.
     Salt, unable to attend the program, wrote in a letter of 15
April: "That the memory of Thoreau, 30 years after his death, should
thus be drawing his readers together, in person and in spirit, in his
native village, is surely sufficient answer to the vain complaint that
he was not ambitious enough 'to engineer for all America.'" Reprinted
in Cameron, 1981a, p. 91.

10 [SANBORN, FRANKLIN BENJAMIN.] "Thoreau and the Walden Woods."
     Boston Herald, 26 May.
     Gives a full account of the damage done to Walden woods by a
recent fire.

11 SALT, HENRY S. "Among the Authors: Henry David Thoreau."
     Vegetarian Review (London), (May), pp. 225–28.
     Discusses the question of whether or not Thoreau was a
vegetarian and decides that he was not a consistent one, for he lived
as others did when he was traveling or at his father's house.

12 A STORY-TELLER. "A Concord Ghost Story." Time and the Hour, 11
     July, pp. 14–16.
     Relates a Louisa May Alcott story of a new servant at the
Thoreau-Alcott house who had seen a ghost. Miss Alcott's cook reminded
her that Thoreau's mother used to wander around the house in just such
a manner as the servant girl described. She was afraid of fires and
checked each night to see that they were all out.

13 F., W.S. "Thoreau." Inquirer (London), 18 July, pp. 457–58.
     Reviews Salt's revised biography of Thoreau, noting that only
after death do some men become "citizens of the world"; they are no
longer provincial and "belong to mankind." Thoreau was one of these.
Twenty-five years ago he was considered a cultured woodsman and thought
to be a strange character by his neighbors. The more educated

1896

considered him an imitator of Emerson. But, in fact, he was one of a group of extraordinary men of New England, all of whom were "by no means the children of transcendentalism," but were the glory of American literature. Lists the prominent American and English critics who have written about him and agrees with Salt that Thoreau left "a burning message for his fellow men."

14 "The Greenacre School / Mr Sanborn on Likenesses and Differences Between Emerson and Thoreau." Boston Evening Transcript, 15 August, p. 11.
    Considers Emerson more like Plato, with principles, and Thoreau like Socrates, with wisdom. They were philosophers who followed wherever truth lead them.

15 von ENDE, A. "Henry David Thoreau." Beilage zur allgemein Zeitung, 26 August, pp. 1–3.
    Classes Thoreau as the greatest transcendental writer and one who practiced individuality.

16 [SANBORN, FRANKLIN BENJAMIN.] "Literary Descriptions of Monadnoc, Which Has Its Hesiod / Edward Emerson's Illustrated Article / Memories of Thoreau, Emerson and Channing." Springfield Republican, 9 September, p. 5.
    Reviews the September article on Monadnoc in New England Magazine. Describes in poetry a camping expedition that Thoreau and Channing made to the mountain. Notes that Chomondeley's Elizabethan house of Condover Hall in England is for sale. Reprinted in Cameron, 1981a, p. 93.

17 HUBERT, PHILIP G., Jr. "Thoreau's Concord." New-York Daily Tribune, 13 September, p. 9.
    An appreciative view of Thoreau and his place in literary history. Notes that in Concord one hears more of Thoreau than of Emerson or Hawthorne.

18 "Life of Henry David Thoreau." Critic 29 (19 September):172.
    Reviews Salt's revised biography of Thoreau and sees great need for further understanding of him. Notes that one prominent sectarian college calls him a minor author. Does not know whether this is because of bigotry or innocence, "but it shows that the Walden recluse is not only misunderstood, but misrepresented by those who can see no virtue in deviating from the deep ruts worn by unthinking masses."

19 Henry David Thoreau. Literary World 27 (17 October):342–43.
    Appreciative review of Salt's biography of Thoreau.

20 "Poems of Nature." Athenaeum (London), 17 October, pp. 517–18.
        Reviews Poems of Nature. Wonders if Thoreau wrote as a poet.
If so, for the most part he failed.

21 "Early Worcester Days / Emerson, Thoreau and Alcott Regarded as
        Freaks." Worcester (Mass) Telegram, 26 October, p. 8.
        Commenting on the lectures: Thoreau's "humorous,
sarcastic, but ever entertaining talks, rather than lectures, were
received with more favor, but perhaps with less comprehension" than
those of the other two. Reprinted in Cameron, 1980b, p. 264.

22 H[ATHAWAY, SAMUEL?] "To the Editor of the Telegram." Worcester
        (Mass.) Telegram, 29 October.
        Adds more comments to 1896.21 about literary Worcester of
fifty years before. Reprinted in Concord Saunterer, no. 2 (August
1984), pp. 3–6.

23 STANLEY, HIRAM M. "Thoreau as a Prose Writer." Dial 21
        (October):179–82.
        Evaluates Thoreau's place as a writer of prose. Taking the
works one by one, he finds them all wanting but does feel that "Wild
Apples" is a perfectly sound essay. Concludes with: "We may say with
confidence that Thoreau's place, though small, is secure and permanent;
he occupies a distinct but minor niche in the eternal Pantheon of Art."
Reprinted in Glick, 1969, pp. 130–38.

24 WOLFE, THEODORE. "Literary Landmarks of Concord." Romance,
        November.
        Describes Thoreau's Concord haunts and homes.

25 [SANBORN, FRANKLIN BENJAMIN.] "Thoreau, Newcomb, Brook Farm."
        Springfield Republican, 2 December, p. 5.
        Reviews the two-volume edition of Cape Cod with Amelia Watson
illustrations.

26 COOKE, GEORGE W. "The Two Thoreaus." Independent 48 (10
        December):1671–72.
        Interrogates local residents who knew Thoreau to discover why
some were admirerers and some detractors and gives the results of his
study. Finds that there are two Thoreaus in the minds of those who
knew him. Tells why both opinions are held. Relates the time Thoreau
was to speak on the day John Brown was hanged.

27 "The Listener." Boston Evening Transcript, 19 December, p. 17.
        Comments on a letter from a lady about the effect that
Thoreau's Cape Cod had on her Cape Cod neighbors, remarking that it was
"as good a book as anyone could write who derived his impressions
wholly from what he had seen from the top of the stage-coach in a

1896

rainstorm." Notes that the homes are now better kept up than in Thoreau's day. Reprinted in Cameron, 1977, p. 119-20.

28 "Thoreau's Cape Cod in Colors." Critic 29 (19 December):402.
     Compliments the printer of the book on the excellence of the color reproductions of Amelia Watson's watercolor paintings of Cape Cod.

29 SANBORN, F[RANKLIN] B[ENJAMIN]. "The Two Thoreaus." Independent 48 (31 December):5.
     Refutes a story in 1896.26, which said that he advised Thoreau that it would not be a good idea to speak in the vestry of the church on the day John Brown was hanged. This was not true as there was no meeting that day in the vestry but a well-advertised one announced a week or two in advance and he, Sanborn, was one of the planners of the meeting. The meeting referred to by Mr. Cooke was perhaps one held at a time when Sanborn was out of town and knew nothing about it until several days later.

30 "Cape Cod." Unitarian, (December).
     Brief appreciation of two-volume set of Cape Cod.

31 TORREY, BRADFORD. "Thoreau." Atlantic Monthly 78 (December):822-32.
     Analyses Thoreau's writings and character, commenting that those who do not care for an occasional bit of paradox or some exaggeration should leave him alone.

32 ABBOTT, CHARLES C[ONRAD]. Notes of the Night and Other Sketches. New York: Century, pp. 215-24.
     Does not consider either Emerson or Lowell competent to make an assessment of Thoreau as neither championed simplicity or sincerity.

33 FIELDS, ANNIE. "Glimpses of Emerson." In Authors and Friends. Boston: Houghton, Mifflin, pp. 68-71.
     Notes that Thoreau's sister, Sophia, added some personal letters after Emerson had completed his editing. Emerson was not happy with the additions, remarking "You have spoiled my Greek statue."

34 IRISH, FRANK V. "Henry D. Thoreau." In American and British Authors. Columbus, Ohio: Frank V. Irish, pp. 134-41.
     Sketches Thoreau's life, noting his friends, listing his principal writings, and quoting critical assessments of others. Several inaccuracies (e.g., "he was carried by loving hands and laid to rest on a hillside in Sleepy Hollow"). [He was moved to that cemetery a few years after his death.]

35 JORDON, DAVID STARR. "The Last of the Puritans." In The Story
    of the Innumerable Company and Other Sketches. San Francisco:
    Whitaker & Ray, pp. 177-201.
        Prints an address on Thoreau and John Brown delivered in 1892
at the California State Normal School at San Jose. Reprinted in
Imperial Democracy (New York: D. Appleton, 1899), pp. 277-93.

36 MABIE, HAMILTON WRIGHT. Essays on Nature and Culture. New York:
    Dodd, Mead, p. 121.
        Comparing their knowledge of nature's habits, believes that
Emerson learned more from her than Thoreau did.

37 MATTHEWS, BRANDER. "Henry David Thoreau." In An Introduction to
    the Study of American Literature. New York: American Book, pp.
    184-93.
        Brief outline of Thoreau's life, with comments on his major
writings. Contains a facsimile of a Thoreau letter to H.G.O. Blake
dated 14 October 1854.

38 PATTEE, FRED LEWIS. "Henry David Thoreau." In A History of
    American Literature. Boston: Silver, Burdett, pp. 221-27.
        Notes that Thoreau's boyhood was similar to Whittier's, being
both unliterary and unencouraging. Reviews the two books published
during his lifetime. Thinks that his prose shows the strong influence
of Emerson but believes that the reverse is also true.

39 SALT, HENRY S. Life of Henry David Thoreau. Great Writers
    Series. London: Walter Scott, 208 pp.; with Thoreau
    bibliography by John P. Anderson.
        Revises 1890.27, omitting many Thoreau quotations and adding
important addenda and corrigenda.

40 SMYTH, ALBERT H. Bayard Taylor. American Men of Letters Series.
    Boston: Houghton, Mifflin, pp. 74, 80.
        Notes that while Taylor was editor of the Union Magazine
Greeley came to him with a Thoreau manuscript and asked him to publish
it. Also mentions Thoreau's trip to Fire Island to check on the
drowning of Margaret Fuller Ossoli.

41 TAPPAN, LUCY. "Henry David Thoreau." In Topical Notes on
    American Authors. Boston: Silver, Burdett, pp. 143-58.
        Biographical sketch comments on his character, temperament,
and personal appearance. Lists his various appellations and some
tributes to him.

42 WILIAMS, HOWARD. "Thoreau and the Simple Life." In The Ethics
    of Diet. Manchester, England: F. Pitman, pp. 231-33.

1896

States that Graham, Greeley, and Thoreau were the best
converts to the superiority of nature's diet. Thoreau was foremost
among those advocating a return to "a less unnatural manner of life."
He was remarkable because of his "magnetic attraction--derived from his
sympathy and from his association with them in his hermit-life--
exercised by him over the non-human races, which gives him something of
a pythagorean character, and a unique position among 'naturalists.'"
He was a food reformer and encouraged the use of bloodless food.

43 WILSON, ANNIE E. Compendium of United States History and
    Literature. Boston: D.C. Heath, p. 44.
    Lists Thoreau as a writer of Walden and other books.

                              1897

1 CHAMBERLIN, JOSEPH EDGAR. "Memorials of American Authors."
   Atlantic Monthly 79 (January):68-69.
       Recounts a visit to Thoreau's cairn bringing thoughts of
those who had laid a stone on it: Buroughs, Torrey, Brewster, Faxon,
and possibly Whitman. Believes that the cabin was "splintered away by
souvenir-gatherers" and hopes that the cairn will not be removed by
farmers for barnyard walls. Would like to see a Thoreau memorial on
the Concord Common.

2 Review of Authors and Friends, by Annie Fields. Critic 27 (20
   February):123.
       Refutes the statement that Emerson's essay on immortality
was written because of the early loss of his friend Thoreau. Notes
that Miss Emerson said that a great part of the essay was written
before Thoreau died.

3 THIDE, OLIVIA. "Thoreau's Unpaid Occupation." New York Bachelor
   of Arts 4 (February):65-70.
       Recounts in a pleasing manner some of Thoreau's daily
activities in the woods.

4 TRYON, KATE. "Thoreau's Hill." Boston Daily Advertiser, 23
   March.
       Describes her trip to Fairhaven Hill and to "Thoreau's Seat"
overlooking the Concord River. Notes that Thoreau considered building
his cabin on this site.

5 Review of "Cheerful Yesterdays," by Higginson, in the April 1897
   Atlantic Monthly. Critic 27 (3 April):237,
       Notes the decline in popularity of Whipple--thought at one
time to be a second Macaulay--and the continuing growth in
international fame of "the eccentric and unsuccessful Thoreau" in spite
of his condemnation by Lowell and others.

6   SANBORN, F[RANKLIN] B[ENJAMIN]. "Thoreau and Emerson." Forum
    23 (April):218-227.
        Compares Emerson with Thoreau and finds that there are wide
differences. Comments on the increasing fame of Thoreau, who
apparently never was concerned about popularity.

7   HURST, Bishop JOHN F. "Historic Concord." Chautauguan 25
    (June):266-373, passim.
        Comments briefly on Thoreau in relation to Concord.

8   HUBERT, PHILLIP G., Jr. "At Thoreau's Pond." Book Buyer 15
    (July):549-57.
        Records a visit to Walden Pond, with thoughts about Thoreau.

9   "The Greenacre Lectures." Boston Evening Transcript, 14 August,
    p. 13.
        Reviews Sanborn's talk "Walks and Talks with Emerson and
Thoreau." Notes that of the five Concord walkers, Emerson, Channing,
Alcott, Hawthorne, and himself, Thoreau was probably the most social.
Reprinted in Cameron, 1980a, pp. 101-2.

10 [SANBORN, FRANKLIN BENJAMIN.] "Thoreau and Whitman Compared as
    Writers." Springfield Republican, 26 August, p. 5.
        Finds an increasing audience for both Whitman's and Thoreau's
writings in spite of their great differences in style, the former
striking out on a style of his own, while the latter used the old and
new English writings as models. Reprinted in Cameron, 1981a, p. 101.

11 MABIE, HAMILTON WRIGHT. "John Burroughs." Century 32
    (August):560-68.
        In comparing Thoreau to Burroughs, Mabie writes that
Burroughs, like Thoreau, is strictly indigenous; "he could not have
grown in any other soil. . . . Of the two, Thoreau had the more
formal education; but Burroughs shows keener susceptibility to
formative influences of all kinds."

12 "Memories of Thoreau. Unpublished Anecdotes of New England's
    Anti-Puritan Author and Naturalist." Truth Seeker, 20 November,
    p. 144.
        C.H. Greene relates some unpublished stories about Thoreau as
told to him by Sophia Thoreau. Describes Thoreau's attic room but
feels that the readers would know that the books did not come from a
luxurious appointed study. Notes that an English admirer has written a
biography of Thoreau, making three formal histories of the person who
had problems finding readers for his writings when he was alive.
Discusses Thoreau's religion deciding that no one "could possibly
conclude that he was a Christian. There is much better reason to think
him a pantheist. . . . He was the antithesis of the Puritans, and his

1897

works are the classics which will help clear New England's mud under
which such men as the Edwardses and Mathers and other Puritans buried
it."

   13 "Memories of Thoreau, Recalled by Ralph Waldo Emerson's Son."
       Brooklyn Daily Eagle, 30 November.
           Reviews a lecture by Edward Emerson given at the Brooklyn
   Institute.

   14 HOWE, M.A. DE WOLFE. "Emerson and Concord." Bookman 6
       (November):203–13.
           Seeking after transcendental truth led Thoreau to his stay at
   Walden Pond. Notes that Whittier could not see much virtue in his
   Walden experiment, which proved "that if a man is willing to sink
   himself into a woodchuck he can live as cheaply as that quadruped."
   Emerson, however, knew him better. Reprinted in 1898.26.

   15 PERRY, JENNETTE BARBOUR. "Between Books." Boston Evening
       Transcript, 1 December.
           Comments on Thoreau, noting the publication of a two-volume
   edition of Walden.

  *16 [SANBORN, FRANKLIN BENJAMIN.] "Henry Heine and Henry Thoreau."
       Springfield Republican, 22 December.
           Source: Allen, p. 137.

   17 MASON, DANIEL GREGORY. "The Idealistic Basis of Thoreau's
       Genius." Harvard Monthly 25 (December):82–93.
           Considers Thoreau an ideal literary character to analyze
   because all of his various sides have not been equally presented. More
   and more he is heard of as a naturalist, less and less as a misanthrope, but little is written about him as a philosopher of life. This
   invites examination. He was intent on following his conscience in
   search of truth, and this led his critics to consider him odd and
   sometimes fanatical. Another quality was his humor, which was
   different from ordinary humor but "transpiersing keenly all shams and
   surfaces." "The basis of Thoreau's idealism was an indomitable probity
   of mind. He had the keenness of sense which penetrates instantaneously
   the mask of appearance, to discover the nucleus of the actuality
   within." Reprinted in Cameron, 1980b, pp. 71–76.

   18 ADAMS, OSCAR FAY. A Dictionary of American Authors. Boston:
       Houghton, Mifflin, pp. 380–81.
           Brief biography of Thoreau.

   19 ARNOLD, SARAH LOUISE, and CHARLES B. ARNOLD "The Battle of the
       Ants." In Stepping Stones to Literature. New York: Silver,
       Burdett, pp. 46–49.

One-paragraph comment on Thoreau followed by the above excerpt from Walden.

20 BACON, EDWIN M. <u>Walks and Rides in the Country Round about</u>
    <u>Boston</u>. Boston and New York: Houghton, Mifflin, pp. 187, 207.
    Describes the location of Thoreau's home at Walden Pond.

21 BATES, KATHERINE LEE. "Henry David Thoreau." In <u>American</u>
    <u>Literature</u>. New York: Macmillan, pp. 260–65.
    Believes that Thoreau went to Walden not as a protest against
society but because he needed solitude to prepare for his life as an
author. Notes the posthumous books. "Thoreau is still the Only. Not
the best of his disciples, not John Burroughs, can reach his upper
notes."

22 BURROUGHS, JOHN. "Henry David Thoreau." In <u>Library of the</u>
    <u>Worlds's Best Literature</u>. Edited by Charles Dudley Warner. 30
    vols. New York: R.S. Peale & J.A. Hill, 25:14871–908.
    Places Thoreau in the second order of American writers.
Claims that he lacks too many qualities to be a first-order author.

23 DALL, CAROLINE H. <u>Transcendentalism in New England: A Lecture</u>.
    Boston: Roberts Brothers, pp. 20–21, 31.
    In the transcendentalist view, there is a danger with such men
as Thoreau that the individual's eccentricities may be attributed to
the philosophy.

24 EMERSON, EDWARD WALDO, ed. <u>A Correspondence Between John</u>
    <u>Sterling and Ralph Waldo Emerson</u>. Boston: Houghton, Mifflin, p.
    80.
    Prints a letter from Emerson to Sterling dated 31 January 1844
mentioning Thoreau as a "youth of genius" who has written for the <u>Dial</u>.

25 ENGEL, EDWARD. <u>Geschichte der englischen Litteratur von den</u>
    <u>Anfangen bis zur Gegenwart. Mit sinem Anhang: Die</u>
    <u>nordamerikanische Litteratur</u>. 4th ed. Leipzig, p. 529.
    Believes Thoreau to be a political nihilist, an American
Rousseau or Diogenes, and a less important writer than Margaret Fuller.

26 FOLEY, P.K. <u>American Authors 1795–1895</u>. Boston: Printed for
    subscribers, pp. 291–92.
    Lists Thoreau's books, with some annotations.

27 KENNEDY, WILLIAM SLOANE. <u>In Portia's Gardens</u>. Boston: Bradlee
    Whidden, pp. 151–53, 212–13, passim.
    Recalls that Thoreau said that he had to walk at least four
miles a day, even when he was ill. Considers the posthumous essays
carelessly edited and improperly titled. None of the greater poets
equals him in minute study of water, "crystalized or fluent." He

1897

excelled in describing the iridescence of ice crystals and the tints
and shadows of fluent water.

28   LATHROP, ROSE HAWTHORNE. Memories of Hawthorne. Boston and New
        York: Houghton, Mifflin, pp. 92-93, 420-21.
           A young girl remembers Thoreau as "usually sad as a pine tree.
His enormous eyes, tame with religious intellect and wild with the
loose rein, making a steady flash in this strange unison of forces,
frightened me dreadfully at first."

29   PAINTER, F.V.N. Introduction to American Literature. Boston:
        Sibley, p. 91.
           Lists Thoreau as a prominent writer and notes some of his
books.

30   STANLEY, HIRAM M. "Thoreau as a Prose Writer." In Essays on
        Literary Art. London: Swan Sonnenschein, pp. 113-26.
           Discusses with approval Thoreau's style of writing.

31   TORREY, BRADFORD. Introduction to Walden. Boston and New York:
        Houghton, Mifflin, pp. ix-xliii.
           Biographical sketch followed by an analysis of Walden, which
concludes that "Time, the ultimate critic," is deciding that Thoreau's
writings will survive.

32   WRIGHT, MARGARET B. Hired Furnished, Being Certain Economical
        Housekeeping Adventures in England. Boston: Roberts Brothers,
        pp. 126-37.
           Gives information on Thoreau's Jersey relatives.

                                1898

1   JONES, SAMUEL A. "Henry D. Thoreau." Ann Arbor (Mich.)
        Washtennan Evening Times, 10 February.
           Reports on a paper read by Dr. Jones before the Unity Club,
in which he corrected some mistaken ideas regarding Thoreau.

2   "Walden." Boston Evening Transcript, 26 February.
        Verse.

3   HOAR, GEORGE F[RISBIE]. "A Boy of Sixty Years Ago." Youth's
        Companion, 24 March.
           Reminisces about when Thoreau was his school teacher. He took
many walks with him and was his friend until his death. Reprinted in
Hoar, Autobiography of Seventy Years, 2 vols. (New York: Charles
Scribner's Sons, 1903), 1:70-72.

                                126

4   J[ONES], S[AMUEL] A. "Vox Clamantis in Deserto." <u>Inlander</u> 8
    (March):222–30.
        Reviews the Holiday Edition of <u>Walden</u>.

5   "Egotism as Taught by Thoreau." <u>Eagle and the Serpent</u> 2 (15
    April):18.
        The magazine is "dedicated to the philosophy of life as
enunciated by Nietzsche, Emerson, Stirner, Thoreau and Goethe."
Contains a page of Thoreau quotations.

6   [SANBORN, FRANKLIN BENJAMIN.] "Walton Ricketson Has Made a Bust
    of an Idealized Thoreau." <u>Springfield Republican</u>, 18 April, p.
    12.
        Considers the bust more poetic and youthful than Thoreau is
remembered, "yet true to his essential character."

7   Obituary of H.G.O. Blake. <u>Worcester</u> (Mass.) <u>Daily Spy</u>, 19 April.
        Sketches Blake's life, noting incorrectly that he was the
author of the <u>Life of Thoreau</u> [perhaps referring to the season books],
and <u>Thoreau's Thoughts</u>, which was edited by him. Reprinted in Cameron,
1958, pp. 275–76.

8   "Thoreau's Friend: Death of Harrison Gray Otis Blake."
    <u>Worcester</u> (Mass.) <u>Evening Gazette</u>, 19 April, p. 4.
        Blake's obituary notes much about his relationship with
Thoreau.

9   "Death of Harrison Gray Otis Blake, Thoreau's Friend, One of the
    Concord School." <u>Worcester</u> (Mass.) <u>Evening Gazette</u>, 21 April, p.
    4.
        Notes that Blake kept a diary in which he recorded his trips
with Thoreau. Lists the books that he edited from the Thoreau
journals.

10 "The Thoreau Journal Goes to E. Harlow Russell, Literary
    Executor." <u>Worcester</u> (Mass.) <u>Evening Gazette</u>, 25 April.
        In his will dated 5 December 1896 Blake left Thoreau's manu-
scripts to Russell, but the income from royalties from the books was
left to George S. Thatcher of Bangor, Maine.

11 MASON, DANIEL GREGORY. "Harrison G.O. Blake, '35 and Thoreau."
    <u>Harvard Monthly</u> 26 (May):87–95.
        Relates Blake's life after leaving Harvard; notes his work on
Thoreau's manuscripts. Reprinted in Cameron, 1980b, pp. 76–79.

12 [SANBORN, FRANKLIN BENJAMIN.] "Death of Parker Pillsbury / His
    Days in Concord at the Thoreaus." <u>Springfield Republican</u>, 18
    July, p. 12.

1898

Recalls that Pillsbury was a frequent visitor at the Thoreau home. It was to him that Thoreau, in his final illness, replied "One world at a time" when asked about future life. Reprinted in Cameron, 1981a, p. 12.

13 LIVINGSTON, L.S. "The First Books of Some American Authors."
     Bookman 8 (September):38–43.
     Tells the story of the return of the unsold copies of A Week on the Concord and Merrimack Rivers and the reissue by Ticknor and Fields. Feels that there is now little interest among collectors of first editions of Thoreau's works, the highest auction price being but $14.50.

14 PENNIWILL, EUNICE V. "Henry David Thoreau." Self Culture,
     September, pp. 57–61.
     Considers that Americans know too little about Thoreau in this day of short-story writing and novels. Recommends that readers look into his books to learn of his restful and quiet life. Notes his biographies by Sanborn and Channing. Calls George Minot his vivacious uncle. He read Goldsmith and Irving, and their influence is evident in his writings. Remarks on his friendship with Emerson, Channing, Alcott, and Ricketson.

15 S[ALT], H.S. "Thoreau Illustrated." Saturday Review 86
     (5 November):600–601.
     Appreciative review of the newly published two-volume illustrated Walden. Considers the Torrey introduction as unnecessary, arguing that the book needs no introduction.

16 [MACDONALD, E.M.] "Another Pioneer Gone." Truth Seeker, 19
     November.
     Notes the death of Calvin Harlow Greene, thought to be the last person to correspond with Thoreau.

17 J[ONES], S[AMUEL] A[RTHUR]. "Thoreau's Incarceration (as Told by
     His Jailer)." Inlander 9 (December):96–103.
     Jailer Sam Staples tells the complete story of Thoreau's jail experience. Reprinted in Thoreau Society Booklet, no. 4 (July 1946), 8 pp.

18 ABBOTT, CHARLES C. The Freedom of the Fields. Philadelphia:
     J.B. Lippincott, pp. 20, 59–60, 116–17.
     Quotes Thoreau that "Nature gets thumbed like an old spelling-book" but does not agree that the public studies this spelling-book. Few like Thoreau can get the pleasures of a quiet evening and be glad that they are living. That some of his critics could not is evident by their misconceptions of the man.

19 BROWN, THEO. Letters of Theo. Brown. Selected by Sarah Brown.
    Worcester: Putnam, Davis, pp. 45, 53, 56, 79.
    Comments on Brown's friendship with Thoreau.

20 BROWNSON, HENRY F. Orestes A. Brownson's Early Life: From 1803
    to 1844. Detroit: H.F. Brownson, pp. 204–5.
        Prints a Thoreau letter of 30 December 1837 to Brownson asking
for assistance in obtaining employment. Reprinted in Harding, 1958,
pp. 19–20.

21 COOKE, GEORGE WILLIS, ed. Early Letters of George Wm. Curtis to
    John S. Dwight. New York: Harper & Bros., 294 pp.
    Comments on Emerson and Thoreau.

22 GRISWOLD, HATTIE TYNG. "Henry David Thoreau." In Personal
    Sketches of Recent Authors. Chicago: A.C. McClurg, pp. 298–315.
        Biographical sketch together with extracts from Thoreau's
prose and poetry to demonstrate his personal feelings. Particular
attention is given to his thwarted love life, maintaining that if he
had been successful in his love it might have changed his whole life.

23 [GRISWOLD, W.M.], ed. Passages from the Correspondence and Other
    Papers of Rufus W[ilmot] Griswold. Cambridge, Mass.: W.M.
    Griswold, pp. 99, 207–213
        Prints Emerson's letter of 25 September 1841 to Griswold
recommending some of Thoreau's poems that were published in the Dial.
Notes that some of these poems were signed "D.H.T" by mistake. Also
prints letters from Horace Greeley asking Griswold to publish Thoreau's
writings, with comments from Julian Hawthorne and Sanborn.

24 HIGGINSON, THOMAS WENTWORTH. Cheerful Yesterdays. Boston:
    Houghton, Mifflin, 374 pp.
        Recounts the time when he tried to get Judge Hoar to persuade
Thoreau's sister to print Thoreau's journals. The judge heard some of
the plea and said, "But you have left unsettled the preliminary
question, Why should anyone care to have Thoreau's journals put in
print?" (p. 170).

25 HIGGINSON, THOMAS WENTWORTH. "Henry David Thoreau." In American
    Prose. Edited by George Rice Carpenter. New York: Macmillan,
    pp. 333–57.
        Defends Thoreau against Lowell's criticism and proves his
increasing fame by telling of a Thoreau letter that sold at auction for
$27.50. One by Hawthorne sold at the same price, one by Longfellow for
$4.50, and one by Holmes for $3.00, each being fine autograph letters.

26 HOWE, M.A. DE WOLFE. American Bookmen. New York: Dodd, Mead,
    295 pp.

1898

Richard Monchton Milnes (not yet Lord Houghton) remarks in a letter to Hawthorne that Leaves of Grass is in the same category as the Thoreau's books, "which you introduced me to, and which are so little known and valued here" (p. 230). Reprinted from 1897.14.

27 NOBLE, CHARLES. Studies in American Literature. New York: Macmillan, pp. 187, 314, 319–21, 333–36, 368.
Discusses Lowell's criticism of Thoreau. Considers that Lowell gives him no general praise nor general condemnation but does help to comprehend Thoreau. Gives a brief biography and Thoreau extracts.

28 PANCOAST, HENRY S. An Introduction to American Literature. New York: Henry Holt, pp. 165, 168, 200–201.
Brief mentions of Thoreau, calling him "Emerson's eccentric disciple" and "strange, sly hunter of the woods."

29 POWELL, LYMAN P. Historic Towns of New England. New York: G.P. Putnam's Sons, 399 pp. passim.
Comments on Thoreau and his part in the New England scene.

30 SANBORN, KATE. "Bachelor Authors as Types." In My Favorite Lectures of Long Ago. Boston: Privately printed, pp. 75–77.
Describes Thoreau as a good example of a bachelor author.

31 SKINNER, CHARLES M. With Feet to the Earth. Philadelphia: J.B. Lippincott, pp. 58–59.
Relates that as they were riding on the Fitchburg Railroad Emerson pointed out Walden Pond, where Thoreau's hut stood.

1899

1 [SANBORN, FRANKLIN BENJAMIN.] "Music and Transcendentalism." Springfield Republican, 25 January.
Notes the publication of Some Unpublished Letters of Henry D. and Sophia E. Thoreau.

2 SALT, HENRY S. "Froude to Thoreau." Academy (London) 56 (11 March):300–306.
Reviews Some Unpublished Letters of Henry D. and Sophia E. Thoreau. Gives a brief history of the publication of A Week on the Concord and Merrimack Rivers. Believes that this book will appeal more to Thoreau students than to the general public.

3 CARRINGTON, CARROLL. "Trying to Live the Life of Thoreau." San Francisco Examiner (Sunday Supplement), 12 March.

Reports of a man named Peckham living in Concord, California, who claimed that he had walked and talked with Thoreau and showed a letter to him from Thoreau. The letter proved to be a modified copy of one sent to Parker Pillsbury. Reprinted in part in TSB, no. 149 (Fall 1979), pp. 3–4.

4 TORREY, BRADFORD. "Writers that Are Quotable." Atlantic Monthly 83 (March):411.
    Partially answers Lowell's criticism of Thoreau and concludes that there are some who feel his chance of immortality is higher than that of either Emerson or Hawthorne.

5 W., K.M. "Thoreau and His Teaching." Inquirer (London), 23 September, pp. 603–4.
    Believes Emerson's "The Transcendentalist" does not recognize the idealist he portrays is one who strives to realize these ideals. "There is something alien, perhaps Oriental about Emerson's 'Transcendentalist' withdrawn from nature." He may have been describing Thoreau. In Thoreau's day orthodoxy was the norm and individuality was repressed, and he could not accept that climate. The criticisms of Lowell, Emerson, and Stephenson are rejected. "To some he seemed a prig, to others he is a prophet."

6 W., K.M. "Thoreau and His Teaching." Pt. 2. Inquirer (London), 30 September, pp. 619–20.
    Asks the question: "What, after all, was Thoreau?" He was not Stephenson's "Skulker." If he withdrew from society it was not because of lack of love for his fellow men but because he wanted "absolute truth and purity of heart," which he could not find in conventional society. He was not irreligious but disagreed with the way Christianity was practiced in his day. He tried to express in his writings what he had learned in living---be simple.

7 [SANBORN, FRANKLIN BENJAMIN.] "Thoreau's Concord Photographed." Springfield Republican, 11 November, p. 11.
    Reports that a photographer has recently been taking pictures of the places mentioned in Thoreau's journals and plans to incorporate them in a new edition of selections from his published works. Reprinted in Cameron, 1981a, p. 112.

8 TORREY, BRADFORD. "Thoreau's Attitude Towards Nature." Atlantic Monthly 64 (November):708–10.
    Considers Thoreau's use of exaggeration a fine art, perhaps not the finest art but most effective as he uses it. Feels that the world has been enriched by his writings.

9 "Reminiscences of Thoreau." Outlook 63 (2 December):815–21.
    An intimate friend of Thoreau's sister, Sophia, recalls many

1899

stories about members of the family. Notes that all had good singing voices and frequently had evening songfests with Sophia playing and at times Henry joining in with his flute. Reprinted in Cameron, 1980b, pp. 79–82.

10 "John Brown's Burial Service / A Concord Liturgy for a Martyr." Concord Middlesex Patriot, 22 December, p. 2.
       Reviews the Concord services of 1859 and Thoreau's part in them, mentioning that he read some verses that he and Emerson had selected.

11 RUSSELL, E. HARLOW. Report of a speech given by Russell before the Unitarian Club. Leominster (Mass.) Daily Enterprise, 28 December.
       Describes Thoreau's physical appearance and his manner of speaking, recalling that he was never charming but always interesting and often entertaining. Reprinted in part in TSB, no. 69 (Fall 1959), pp. 1–2.

12 ABBOTT, CHARLES C. Clear Skies and Cloudy. Philadelphia: J.B. Lippincott, pp. 35, 65, 272, 293.
       Mentions Thoreau's bird calls and other nature notes.

13 ARMIN, ELIZABETH [BEAUCHAMP] GRAFIN VON [ELIZABETH]. The Solitary Summer. New York: Macmillan, pp. 23–26.
       Delights in reading Walden when out of doors and insists that Thoreau "will refuse to give you much pleasure if you try to read him amid the pomp and circumstances of upholstery; but out in the sun, and essentially by this pond, he is delightful, and we spend the happiest hours together, he making statements, and I either agreeing heartily, or just laughing and reserving my opinion till I shall have more ripely considered the thing." [The pond referred to is not Walden but one near her home.]

14 BRONSON, WALTER C. A Short History of American Literature. Boston: D.C. Heath, pp. 210–13.
       Briefly comments on Thoreau's life and his works.

15 CHADWICK, JOHN WHITE. A Life for Liberty. New York: G.P. Putnam's Sons, p. 167.
       Notes that Thoreau's "Autumnal Tints" lecture was always well received.

16 FEDERN, KARL. "Henry David Thoreau." In Essays zur amerikanischen Litteratur. Germany: Halle an der Saale, pp. 141–59.
       Comments on American transcendentalism, with a final chapter on Thoreau and his part in the movement.

17 FISHER, MARY. "Henry David Thoreau." In <u>A General Survey of</u>
    <u>American Literature</u>. Chicago: A.C. McClurg, pp. 286–309.
        Comprehensive review of Thoreau's life and his writings.
Says that Emerson wrote about man's relation to society and nature,
Thoreau about nature and her relation to man. Believes that if either
received inspiration from the other it was Emerson who was the debtor.
He took Thoreau's essays on indifference to material things as a model
of excellence. Concludes that although "we must admit the limitations
and the extravagance of some of Thoreau's opinions, his life is none
the less a fine example of the surpassing beauty and richness of the
intellectual life, in comparison with the meanness and ugly vulgarity
of those lives whose real poverty is in some measure concealed by the
clutter of material luxury, and whose only aim is to conceal it still
more effectively by further accumulations."

18 GAYLEY, CHARLES MILLS, and FRED NEWTON SCOTT. <u>An Introduction to</u>
    <u>the Methods and Materials of Literary Criticism</u>. Boston: Ginn,
    pp. 230, 343.
        Recommends for study page 301 of the 1894 edition of Early
<u>Spring in Massachusetts</u> and page 494 of the same edition of <u>A Week on</u>
<u>the Concord and Merrimack Rivers</u>.

19 HIGGINSON, THOMAS WENTWORTH. <u>Contemporaries</u>. Boston: Houghton,
    Mifflin, 379 pp.
        Uses Thoreau quotations to highlight the characteristics of
some American writers and statesmen.

20 HIGGINSON, THOMAS WENTWORTH. <u>Old Cambridge</u>. New York:
    Macmillan, pp. 34, 58, 67, 191.
        Notes that Judge Hoar could see no reason to publish Thoreau's
journals. Prints a letter of 25 November 1853 from Francis H.
Underwood that states that Thoreau and others were willing to write for
a proposed magazine.

21 JONES, SAMUEL ARTHUR. <u>Some Unpublished Letters of Henry D.</u>
    <u>Thoreau and Sophia E. Thoreau</u>. New York: Marion Press, 86 pp.
        Prints a miscellany of comments with Thoreau's letters to
and from Calvin Greene, Sophia Thoreau, and J.A. Froude.

22 JORDAN, DAVID STARR. "The Last of the Puritans." In <u>Imperial</u>
    <u>Democracy</u>. New York: D. Appleton, pp. 277–93.
        Notes that the adverse critics see only the extravagances and
paradoxes in Thoreau's writings, and miss the beauty that his admirers
see in them.

*23 KNAPP, ELLA A. <u>A Study of Thoreau</u>. Ann Arbor, Mich.:
    University of Michigan.

1899

Not printed but noted here because it was perhaps the first
doctoral dissertaion on Thoreau. Noted in TSB, no. 110 (Winter 1970),
p. 5.

24 KNORTZ, KARL. Ein amerikanischer Diogenes, Henry D. Thoreau.
   Hamburg, 32 pp.
   In two sections: the first lauds Thoreau's attacks on
society's shams; the second compares him with Goethe, Christ, Faust,
and many others.

25 LYMAN, EMILY R., ed. Extracts from Thoreau. Philadelphia: J.B.
   Lippincott, 175 pp.
   The introduction states that the extracts were taken from his
eleven volumes of prose works. "The charm is indefinable." He was
inspired by nature and the noble simplicity of living.

26 MITCHELL, DONALD G. American Lands and Letters: Leather-
   Stocking to Poe's "Raven." New York: Charles Scribner's Sons,
   pp. 271-82.
   Comments that to know Thoreau one must read him "thoroughly,
up and down and across, in every light, every season, every labor. The
truths of nature quiver in his talk, as color quivers on a chameleon."

27 RANDALL, JOHN WITT. Poems of Nature and Life. Edited by Francis
   Ellingwood Abbott. Boston: George H. Ellis, p. 109.
   Prints a letter of 9 January 1857 to Frances Ellingwood Abbot
with Thoreau references.

28 ROBERTS, CHARLES G.D., ed. Introduction to Walden. New York:
   T.Y. Crowell, pp. v-xvi.
   Notes that Thoreau once loved a woman and gave her up for his
brother but is uncertain whether he loved the ecstasy of self-sacrifice
as much as he did the woman.

29 STEVENSON, ROBERT LOUIS. "Preface, by Way of Criticism." In
   Familiar Studies of Men and Books. New York: Charles Scribner's
   Sons, pp. 16-21, 137-73.
   Says that Dr. Japp presented him with a completely new
concept of Thoreau, and he admits that he misrepresented Thoreau in his
first article. The original article is reprinted.

30 STEVENSON, ROBERT LOUIS. The Letters of Robert Louis Stevenson
   to His Family and Friends. Edited by Sidney Colvin. 2 vols. New
   York: Charles Scribner's Sons, 1:443; 2:465.
   Comments on writing the essay on Thoreau and prints the
correspondence with Japp about the essay on Thoreau.

Undated Nineteenth-Century Entries.

1 FITZ, D. THOREAU. "Henry D. Thoreau: Woodland Poet of Lake
  Walden." Unidentified newspaper clipping.
     Verse about Thoreau and his Walden Pond stay.

2 SMITH, ELIZABETH OATES. "An Incident" and "Thoreau."
  Unidentified newspaper clipping pasted in a copy of Walden.
     Two sonnets. the first concerns Smith's first meeting with
Thoreau after she had delivered a lecture; the second extols his love
for nature. Information on this clipping and reprinting of the sonnets
in TSB, no. 110 (Winter 1970), pp. 2-3.

3 "Thoreau Gloving Mrs. Emerson's Hens." Minneapolis Tribune,
  undated clipping.
     An old Concordian tells of knowing Thoreau and of the village
reaction to him. Relates the story that at the instruction of Mrs.
Emerson, Thoreau tied cloth bandages on her hens' feet to keep them
from scratching up her flower garden.

4 Unknown newspaper.
     Reviews Walden, with a note that one of the wealthiest ladies
in Concord fell in love with Thoreau and proposed marriage but he
turned her down, preferring his solitary life.

Index

137

ELLIS, RUFUS, 1865.17;
1866.18
EMERSON, EDWARD WALDO,
1888.15; 1891.2; 1894.13–
16; 1897.13
EMERSON, RALPH WALDO, 1862.3,
24; 1844.12; 1848.3;
1849.14, 28; 1853.1, 2;
1854.1, 6, 16, 17; 1862.3, 7,
24; 1863.13; 1865.11, 20, 28;
1867.1; 1873.4; 1877.2, 5;
1878.8, 16; 1880.18; 1882.2,
9–12, 19–20, 23, 25, 34;
1883.6, 11–12; 1884.5, 7, 9–
10, 16–17; 1885.16; 1886.1,
6; 1887.13; 1888.2, 10, 15;
1889.4, 12; 1890.3, 6, 18;
1891.24; 1892.10–11, 17;
1893.25, 27, 28; 1894.2, 18,
20, 31; 1895.3, 5, 17;
1896.1, 7, 13–14, 32–33;
1897.2, 6, 9, 24; 1898.23;
1899.5, 17
Emerson at Home and Abroad
(Conway), 1882.32
Emerson in Concord, (Emerson)
1888.15
Encyclopedia Britannica,
1888.19
ENGEL, EDWARD, 1897.25
England's Ideal (Carpenter),
1887.14; 1895.27
Essays and Other Writings of
Henry Thoreau (Dircks),
1891.18
Essays on Literary Art
(Stanley), 1897.30
Essays on Nature and Culture
(Mabie), 1896.36
Essays zur amerikanischen
Litteratur (Federn), 1899.16
The Eulogy of Richard
Jefferies (Besant),
1888.13
EVANS, MARIAN. See Eliot,
George
EVERETT, A.N., 1882.28
Excursions
–references to, 1890.9; 1891.26;
1894.35
–reviews of, 1863.5–10, 11–13
Extracts from Thoreau, 1899.25

F., E.M., 1883.1
F., W.S., 1896.13
Familiar Letters
–reference to, 1894.33
–reviews of, 1894.2, 17, 19, 20;
1895.7
Familiar Studies of Men and
Books (Stevenson), 1899.29
FEDERN, KARL, 1899.16
FELTON, CORNELIUS CONWAY,
1849.22
FIELDS, ANNIE, 1881.17; 1896.33;
1897.2
FIELDS, JAMES T[HOMAS],
1877.5; 1880.23; 1881.17
Fifty Years among Authors,
Books and Publishers
(Derby), 1885.10
First Century of the Republic
(Whipple), 1876.7
First Editions of American
Authors (Stone), 1893.26
FISHER, MARY, 1899.17
FITZ, D. THOREAU, undated.1
FLAGG, WILSON, 1872.7;
1880.18; 1881.9, 18
FLUGEL, EWALD, 1889.4
FOLEY, P.K., 1897.26
Foot Notes or Walking as a
Fine Art (Barron), 1875.5
FOSTER, DANIEL, 1852.3
Freedom of the Fields (Abbott),
1898.18
Fresh Fields (Burroughs), 1885.9
From the Easy Chair (Curtis),
1893.24
FROTHINGHAM, OCTAVIUS BROOKS,
1889.9
Fuller, Margaret (Ossoli),
1850.3–5; 1871.3; 1882.17;
1883.11; 1884.19; 1896.40

GAYLEY, CHARLES MILLS, 1899.18
GARNETT, RICHARD, 1888.16
George Eliot's Life (Eliot),
1885.11
A General Survey of American
Literature (Fisher), 1899.17
Geschichte der
nordamerikanischen
Litteratur (Knortz),
1891.23

Index

1878.7; 1887.8
Thoreau, John, Jr., 1842.1
Thoreau, John, Sr., 1887.22;
  1893.6
Thoreau, Sophia, 1876.2
Thoreau: The Poet-Naturalist
  With Memorial Verses
-references to, 1864.1; 1873.3-4
-reviews of, 1873.1, 5-12;
  1874.1, 3, 5-6
"Thoreau and Channing,"
  (Shattuck) 1884.6
"Thoreau and Greeley," 1882.3
"Thoreau and His
  Biographers," (Jones)
  1891.9
"The Thoreau Club Girls,"
  1891.16
Thoreau's Lectures
-advertisements for, 1843.1-2;
  1844.3-8; 1849.1; 1852.4-5;
  1854.14, 26-31, 33-34;
  1855.11; 1856.4-5; 1857.5;
  1858.3; 1859.1, 5-8; 1860.8-
  11
-reviews of, 1843.3; 1848.3-4;
  1849.2-4, 9-10; 1851.1.
  1854.35; 1855.1-3; 1857.1-2;
  1859.4, 10-17; 1860.13, 16-
  17; 1861.1-2
Thoreau's Thoughts, 1890.19, 22;
  1891.1, 6
THOROUGH, TIMOTHY [pseud.],
  1849.5
TOLMAN, GEORGE, 1890.10
Topical Notes on American
  Authors (Tappan), 1896.41
TORREY, BRADFORD, 1896.31;
  1897.31; 1899.4, 8
Transactions of the Literary
  and Historical Society of
  Quebec, 1882.37
Transcendentalism in New
  England: A Lecture (Dall),
  1897.23
"Transportation and Planting
  of Seeds," 1879.12
TREVOR, JOHN, 1893.19
TRIGGS, OSCAR LOVELL, 1893.27
TRYON, KATE, 1895.13, 22; 1897.4

UNDERWOOD, FRANCIS H., 1872.9;

1888.9; 1893.28
UNDERWOOD, SARA A., 1884.2;
  1892.6

The Vanity and Insanity of
  Genius (Sanborn), 1885.14
Von ENDE, A., 1896.15

W., K.M., 1899.5-6
Walden; or, Life in the Woods
-references to, 1854.2-3, 5, 10-
  12, 25; 1855.4, 1855.8-9;
  1868.3; 1877.4; 1880.24;
  1882.23; 1883.3; 1886.3-5;
  1887.7, 14, 22; 1888.3;
  1889.11, 13; 1890.9, 26;
  1892.8, 12; 1893.21; 1894.25,
  30, 38; 1895.1; 1896.43;
  1897.15, 19, 31; 1899.13;
  undated.4
-reviews of, 1854.6-9, 13, 15-
  24, 36-37; 1855.5, 7; 1856.1;
  1857.6; 1862.12, 20; 1864.3;
  1865.23; 1898.4, 15
The Wanderer: A Short
  Colloquial Poem (Channing),
  1871.8
WARD, ANNIE J. 1895.21
WARREN, INA RUSSELLE, 1895.16
"Warrington" Pen-Portraits
  (Robinson), 1877.13
WASSON, DAVID ATWOOD, 1863.2
WATKINS, MILDRED CABELL, 1894.41
WATTS-DUNTON, THEODORE,
  1882.27
WAYLEN, HECTOR, 1895.10
A Week on the Concord and
  Merrimack Rivers
-references to, 1851.2; 1854.1;
  1856.2; 1866.14; 1868.1, 4;
  1882.23; 1889.8; 1891.7;
  1894.9, 39; 1898.13; 1899.2,
  18
-reviews of, 1849.13-16, 19-21,
  23, 25-30; 1850.1-2; 1854.32;
  1855.5; 1864.4, 15;
  1865.23; 1867.5; 1877.13;
  1889.3
WEISS, JOHN, 1865.14; 1874.10
WELSH, ALFRED H., 1882.38
WHIPPLE, EDWIN PERCY, 1876.7;
  1882.25; 1887.23-24

146